The Jesus Resolution

Casandra Martin

Published by 21st Century Christian

ISBN-13: 978-0-89098-344-7
eISBN: 978-0-89098-955-5

The Jesus Resolution

THE JESUS RESOLUTION

We serve a God of fresh starts and new beginnings. He promises that His mercies will be new every morning and that U-turns make heaven erupt with joy. Each year brings different opportunities to make resolutions. We make resolutions on New Year's Day, birthdays, anniversaries, at the beginning of the school year, and when the seasons change. In these resolution moments, we delight in the clean slate that they offer us. Resolutions inspire us to start over and begin anew.

Amid all the resolutions we make about our health, our relationships, our work, and our play, I want to challenge you to join me in a resolution that is at the heart of who God is and who He calls us to be. The Jesus Resolution.

The Jesus Resolution is the purpose for which we were created. It is God's ultimate desire for you. It is the reason behind the cross and the empty tomb. God wants to transform you to look like Jesus. He wants to shape you into a mirror image of Christ. He wants others to look at your life and see His Son. He wants your words to be an echo of His voice. He wants the way you move, work, serve, love, and play to resonate with the person of Jesus.

Paul li*ved* and spoke about The Jesus Resolution. He tells his friends in Corinth, *"For I decided to know nothing among you except Jesus Christ and him crucified"* (I Corinthians 2:2). John writes to his loved ones and says, *"[W]hoever says he abides in him ought to walk in the same way in which he walked"* (I John 2:6).

This is the promise and the challenge that God sets out before us. Be His. Be like His Son. Surrender to His transformation. Not just at church or in spiritual mountaintop moments, but while doing the laundry, washing the dishes, going to the dentist, picking up toys, and heading off to work. He longs for His transformation to penetrate my most ordinary, regular moments in order to show me how extraordinary life can be when I make Jesus the center of everything that I am.

My Jesus Resolution is to immerse myself in Jesus. I want Him to soak into every part of who I am. I want to spend this time learning and surrendering to what it means to walk as Jesus did. I resolve to know nothing except Jesus Christ and Him crucified. I commit to living more fully in the transformation God wants to work within me. Will you join me?

Will you make the commitment today to walk in The Jesus Resolution? Memorize 1 Corinthians 2:2.

I am clumsy. It seems I can't eat without leaving a trail of evidence. This morning it was a delicious apple and cinnamon combination that I was enjoying for breakfast. It fell off my fork and rolled down the front of my clothes. Now there are a series of brown blotches where it tumbled across my front.

I tried to wipe it off. I was more successful at making the stain larger and more spread out than I was in actually getting any of it to come up. I finished eating my meal, determined to take care of the mess when I was done.

My next level of efforts found me wetting a towel and trying to wash the stains out. I scrubbed, thinking that they would quickly disappear. They didn't. I scrubbed harder, against the grain, going back and forth. They faded…a little. I can still see their pathway across my front.

I am sure that my next step will be to try a product whose commercials promise to magically eliminate stains in one single wash. I will put the product on the stains and hold my breath. When the washing machine is finished, I will take the garment out and search for the remnants of the stains. They might still be there. Hopefully, they will be gone. No guarantees.

But that laundry room truth causes me to pause. The ugly brown stains across my shirt are nothing compared to the stain in my soul. Sin leaves its mark on me as surely as food tumbling off my fork. The evidence is clear. It mars the beauty of my heart and disrupts the peace meant to define my soul.

My own clean-up efforts won't work. I can scrub, trying to work harder and harder to get the stain out. It won't budge. I can apply worldly solutions, hoping that they will fulfill the promises that caused me to buy into them in the first place. They won't. There is, however, a solution to my stain problem. *"They have washed their robes and made them white in the blood of the Lamb"* (Revelation 7:14).

My Jesus Resolution today is to be thankful for Jesus' blood. His blood makes me clean. His blood makes me new. I want to plant myself in the shadow of the cross and let the tidal wave of His grace wash over me. I am going to stop trying to cleanse myself and move more deeply into His mercy and faithfulness. I am going to rejoice in the guarantee that comes with surrender – there is no stain too deep, too dark, or too filthy for His blood to cleanse and make new.

Read Psalm 103:10-12. How will you be extraordinarily thankful for the grace He extends to you today?

It had been a very cold couple of days and nights. We had been under hard freeze warnings, and the threat of icy weather kept most people inside. We didn't get the snow we had been hoping for, but a thin coat of ice covered everything.

We live in a place where icicles are a novelty. We stepped outside in the chilly air to take a look. They hung from the branches, from the cars, and from the eaves of the roof. Moisture had left its mark on plants and sidewalks and windows. The temperature hadn't risen above freezing all day, so the ice created its own art even in the middle of the afternoon.

It was a rose bush that caught my attention. There were no icicles hanging off those branches, but the leaves looked shiny. Closer inspection yielded a treasure – an ice leaf. Water had frozen on the leaf, taking its shape as its own. Lifting the ice off the plant revealed a perfectly formed ice leaf. The veins of the leaf were imprinted in the ice. The shape of the ice perfectly mirrored the shape of the leaf. It was a copy of the leaf done entirely in ice.

I marveled as I held it in my hand. Moisture and cold came together to create beauty in an unlikely place. Then I realized I was holding a picture of my heart.

We are supposed to be like that ice leaf. Attached to Jesus, we are meant to take His shape and reflect His image. When people look at us, God wants them to see all the details of Jesus in our lives. He longs for us to mirror His life in every way. As He holds me in His hand, grace and surrender come together to create beauty in an unlikely place—His image in me.

My Jesus Resolution today is to be like an ice leaf. I want the shape of Jesus to be imprinted deep on my heart. I want to cling to Him, holding on to His Word and His love. I want to help others marvel at the possibilities of what walking with God can mean for their own lives.

How will you commit yourself to looking more like Jesus today?

She called during dinner Sunday night. Our daughter's ride home had unraveled and the airwaves were filled with panic. Our daughter is a freshman in college. Some of you read that and smile. Some of you read that with dread. You are both right. She has been gone for three months, and this is going to be her first time to come home. She is so excited. She makes daily announcements of the number of days until THE day. She found a ride, worked out the details, made the adjustments, and was all set to come home. Her desire to come home colors everything she does and fills every conversation. "I can't wait…" starts more sentences than you can imagine, so news of her transportation dilemma hit her hard. "What am I going to do?" she cried. "I want to come home!" Mom and Dad to the rescue. He calmed her down and I started searching for a way. We weighed the options, checked the schedules, worked the details, and pulled out our checkbook. "Don't worry," we said. "You are coming home."

I love the way that my daughter longs for home. We should all have that kind of intense homesickness. She is very clear about the fact that school is not home. She likes college. She enjoys her classes and her friends. Her roommate is great. But it isn't home. We can love so many things about this world, but we must never lose sight of the fact that this is just not home. We also face the same transportation problem. Our own ideas and solutions fall far short of getting us home and, just like my daughter, the answer is found in depending on our Father.

All those are good things to think about. But what intrigues me most are my own feelings. As much as she wanted to come home, I couldn't wait for her to be here. We were more than willing to pay the cost to bring her home. She was counting down days. I counted the hours. Do you think that maybe God is more excited about you coming home than you are? Do you think He longs for it with more intensity than you can imagine? My daughter was focused on her own desire for home, and that was great. Waiting for her gave me a glimpse into the heart of God.

My Jesus Resolution today is to be excited about going home. I am going to take the lessons I have learned from my daughter and set my heart toward home. I am going to remember that this is a great place, but a temporary place. I am going to count on my Father to bring me home. I am going to imagine the delight in God's heart when He hears my anticipation. I have been waiting to go home for a while now. He has been preparing for me to be home since before the world began.

What makes you most long for home?

ONE OF THOSE DAYS

Have you ever had one of those days? I looked at my calendar this morning and just knew it was going to be one of those days. The timeline starts before the crack of dawn, weaving its way through appointments, deadlines, must-dos, need-tos, and things to get through before I even have a chance to catch my breath or check to make sure my shoes match.

It is easy to look at days like today and become discouraged. "It is going to be one of those days" plays like a headline over the horizon of the day. I worry about schedules, meeting deadlines, fulfilling expectations, and just plain old getting enough laundry done so that my kids have clean socks for tomorrow. With worry comes guilt; with guilt comes regret; and regret steals joy and plunders peace.

Jesus has the power to change those "one of those days" days into "Wow! This is one of those days!" days. Days defined by joy. Days drenched with grace. Days where we rub our eyes in wonder, knowing we have stood in His presence and been touched by His love. There is no magic key. It requires shifting our perspective, realigning our hearts, and letting the shadow of the cross color our vision.

Today is going to be one of those days –

- One of those days jam-packed with opportunities to see God at work.
- One of those days filled with blessings and reasons to give thanks.
- One of those days overflowing with occasions to say "I love you."
- One of those days crammed with chances to show His grace to others.

- One of those days wide open with possibilities for praise.
- One of those days bursting with the potential for discovering beauty.
- One of those days made for singing out loud and walking with a grin.
- One of those days shaped for His glory and filled with His presence.

My Jesus Resolution today is to have one of those days. A day in which I look for the possibilities instead of the problems. A day where I delight in the blessings rather than complaining about the burdens. A day where I meet each moment with thanksgiving for all the opportunities I have to go and do and be with others. A day in which I meet the morning with a smile as I look at my calendar and say, "It is going to be one of those days!"

What do you need to embrace in order to have "one of those days"?

Wash me, and I shall be whiter than snow. —**Psalm 51:7b**

It was an ordinary, crazy day. As a young mother, I had spent the hours doing laundry, wiping noses, tying shoes, picking up toys, making dinner, and managing the chaos that characterizes a house filled with children.

For the moment the house was quiet. My husband had the kids out in the backyard trying to run the last bit of energy out of them before it was time to start the bedtime routine. I watched out of the window. Standing by the sink, I washed dishes as I watched them run, laugh, and play.

I wish I could tell you that it was a time in which I soaked in the joy of family and the blessing of this picture of heaven. It wasn't. I regret that I didn't put the soap away, leave the dishes in the sink, and go outside to join them. I didn't. Instead I complained, making a grumpy mess of the moment.

I scrubbed pans, rinsed plates, and mopped milk up off the floor, griping the whole time. Why did I have to wash the dishes? Why did I seem to spend all my time cleaning up other people's messes?

It was in the midst of all my complaining that God spoke very quietly to my heart. The cross is all about cleaning. Cleaning the grime of guilt, the stain of sin, and the ring of rebellion from my soul. His blood washes, scrubs, and sanitizes my heart. Every day, He cleans up messes He didn't make. Every day, He steps in and makes right what I have done wrong. Every day, He washes what I have made dirty. He does it because He loves me. He does it because it allows us to live together. He does it because He knows I am growing and learning how to be His.

My Jesus Resolution today is to see God when I wash the dishes. I am going to let a sink full of water remind me of how He washes all my sins away. I am going to let the soap remind me of the power of His blood. I am going to be thankful for clean dishes and a clean heart. I am going to let the sink be a place of awe and wonder as each mess reminds me of what Jesus is doing for me.

Make the time you spend washing dishes today a time to enjoy the presence of God. Thank Him for washing you, cleansing you, and making you new.

GOING HOME

It had been a long day. I had been away from my family for a couple of days. The airport, I rediscovered, was still a lovely shade of unremarkable grey. The hard plastic chairs didn't provide any sort of comfort. Dragging my suitcase from gate to gate demanded the agility of an athlete. Airline traffic seemed to crawl more slowly than usual. My good hair day had gotten blown away by the wind. My feet hurt, my tummy growled, and I was just plain grumpy. I wanted to go home!

I approached the airline representative at the gate to get my seat assignment, eyeing a chair in the terminal where I could eat my airport sandwich before getting on the plane. I handed the agent my ticket and stood there. And stood there. There was something about the way that she looked at me that made my stomach sink. "I'm sorry," she said. "There are no more seats available on this flight."

My face crumpled. I hadn't even considered the possibility that I couldn't get on the flight. Another long night of being away from home was just about more than I could wrap my heart around. The agent told me that perhaps something would open up. Now it was time to wait.

I waited and prayed. Called home and prayed. Ate my sandwich and prayed. Watched the line and prayed. Finally, they started boarding the plane. They didn't call my name, but I decided to ask one more time. The agent found me a seat. It didn't matter that it was in the middle of the row or at the back of the plane. I was going home.

Sometimes we just want to go home. Home is that place where we are known and loved, comfortable and safe. Home is important, and our Father has a passion for bringing people home. Lost, lonely, dirty, hurting, smelly, distracted, or angry – it doesn't matter where we have been. It matters what direction we are headed in right now.

My Jesus Resolution today is to remember how good it feels to go home. I want that same sense of longing, that same desire for the familiar, that same anticipation to soak into my day. I want to imagine how good it is going to be when we get to our heavenly home – to see the faces so dear to me, to know I am loved beyond imagining, to be in the presence of Jesus. God has already paid the price and made a way for me to come home. Are you headed for home?

Remember a time when you just couldn't wait to get home. How will you live with that same kind of anticipation for heaven today?

For I am sure that neither death nor life, nor angels nor rulers, nor things present nor things to come, nor powers, nor height nor depth, nor anything else in all creation, will be able to separate us from the love of God in Christ Jesus our Lord. — **Romans 8:38-39**

It is just a little thing, really. A Post-it® note stuck to the mirror. I left the note as a reminder for my husband of a chore that needed to be handled. When I came back through, it had been moved to my side of the mirror. Drawn on top of the words was a small heart. Just a note back telling me that it was taken care of. But it was more than that. It told me that I was taken care of. That I was loved. That I was important and special. He could have left a check mark or just completed the task and moved on. I would have been fine. Instead, he filled the moment with more.

God is like that. How many times a day does God not only answer our prayers, but infuse the moment with His love? How often does He leave little reminders that He cares around for us to find? He doesn't have to. We would be fine. But He wants us to know the depth of His love, to be enfolded in the breadth of His passion, to experience the intensity of His notice. We have to learn to see the notes. We often pass by and fail to see His fingerprints on our day. Love notes go unread. Reminders that we are cherished go unnoticed.

My Jesus Resolution today is to look around for my love note. It is there. God always leaves His heart for us to find. It may be in an unusual place. It might be attached to something so ordinary that we have to really look to see it. Keep your eyes and your heart open today. And don't be surprised if you find little reminders of God's love stamped everywhere you look.

Look for a love note from God today.

The Jesus Resolution

PLUGGED IN

I am not a very mechanically-inclined person. One day, my computer wasn't working, and I was frustrated. I had tried everything. I pressed buttons, flipped switches, opened drives, even sang it a song, but nothing worked. My computer and I spend a lot of time together, so I was feeling a little desperate by the time I called my husband. Now understand that my husband is a computer guy. No, really; it's his job. In fact, at work they call him "The Wizard." So it was with high hopes that I called him, expecting that out of his technical wizardry, he would be able to conjure the right sequence of buttons to push to make my computer come alive. He did. It was a little embarrassing. "Is it plugged in?" After a second of being defensive, I looked down under my desk, and sure enough, the cord laid innocently next to the power strip. I connected the cord, pressed the power button, and my computer sprang to life. "Always start with the basics," he said. "It is amazing how many times people think they have a big problem, when all they need to do is connect to the power source."

In Ephesians 1:15-23, Paul prays that those who read his letter will be filled with power. He wants the power of gratitude to take deep hold in our lives and make our hearts tender to the truths of God. He longs for our eyes to be opened to the heart of God so that we can experience the rich hope to which He calls us in Christ. He lays out in full detail the scope of the power that is ours. Nothing less than the power of the resurrection is at work in our lives. As he finishes his prayer, he reminds us of the necessity of being plugged in to the power source.

Jesus is the ultimate Power Source. The world offers us many power sources from which to choose. They all glitter and sparkle, trying to capture our attention and hold our interest. Yet, in an astounding declaration, Paul reminds us that all things have been put under Christ's feet. Jesus outshines all the other sources of power in this world. They are like birthday candles next to the sun.

My Jesus Resolution today is to plug into the power of Jesus. I want to be connected to Him, dependent on His grace and tethered to His love. I want the power of the resurrection to transform me from the inside out. I don't want to rely on substandard sources of power, whether my own strength or the power sources of the world. Being plugged in means opening my heart to the power He wants to surge through every part of my life, letting others see the mighty strength of the cross illuminated in me.

What can you do today to be better connected to Jesus and His power?

Excerpt from
Women Opening the Word
Immeasurably More

COOKIES PLEASE

His dad came to pick him up. We had spent the afternoon playing with our little friend, and smiles covered everyone's faces. Basketballs bounced, footballs were thrown, and spaghetti sauce graced the tablecloth, floor, and a couple of sleeves. Trains made their way across the tracks, and the aroma of chocolate chip cookies filled the air.

The cookies were there by special request. A couple of days before, I mentioned that I was headed to the grocery store and my little friend told me that I needed to buy chocolate chips. "We need to make chocolate chip cookies." Having previously been at my house when I didn't have all the necessary ingredients, he wanted to make sure I was prepared. Chocolate chips went on the list.

We made the cookies and enjoyed them (after the proper amount of vegetables, of course). We were putting his jacket on and zipping up his backpack when he looked at me and said, "Can I take some cookies home with me? Two? No, I need five."

Embarrassed, his dad tried to redirect his request. My boys laughed. I headed to the kitchen. Five cookies in a bag for a little boy I love.

I gave him cookies, but he gave me so much more. Another mirror into the heart of God. He wanted something and he asked. No worries; no "how will this look?"; no "should I or shouldn't I?"; no "is this too much?" He knew my heart. He trusted. He asked and he received.

God wants me to ask with all the innocence, trust, faith, wisdom, and sincerity of a child asking for cookies. My little friend didn't worry about asking for too much. He trusted that my answer would be the very best for him. God wants me to stand in his shoes. Trust His heart and ask with boldness.

My Jesus Resolution today is to set my worry down and ask. God delights in me even more than we delight in the children who bless our lives. Joy flows from bringing my requests to God, looking up, and asking Him to move. Courage comes from knowing that He will only give me His very best. Today I am going to be bold. Today I am going to remember that God is prepared to fill me with Himself. All I have to do is ask.

Write Luke 11:9-10
on your heart today.

The Jesus Resolution

HAPPY _____ DAY!

Today I am taking my inspiration from my eight-year-old nephew. Every morning, he gets up announcing what he is celebrating about the day. Yesterday, for example, was "Happy Cousins Day!" because he so loves to be with his family. Another day might be "Happy Swimming Day!" or "Happy Pizza Day!" I love the fact that he can find something to celebrate every day. No matter what is on the agenda, what has happened the day before, how he feels, or what the weather is like, he wakes up anticipating joy. As he said, "I am good at joy."

In that statement, I hear the whisper of God. "I am good at joy," He says. It is joy He wants to share with us. His desire is to listen to our hearts awaken each morning anticipating the joy that He will pour into the day. He longs for us to search the horizon of every moment, finding reasons to celebrate. Celebrate His presence. Celebrate His love. Celebrate His grace. Celebrate His goodness. Celebrate joy.

Psalm 118:24 says, *"This is the day that the LORD has made; let us rejoice and be glad in it."* The facts that God made this day, and filled it with possibilities to meet Him, hear His voice, experience His mercy, and be enfolded in His love are reasons to celebrate. He tells us that we can rejoice. Not everything in our day will be good, but we can celebrate the truth that in everything God is good.

My Jesus Resolution today is to be good at joy. I am going to search for something to celebrate, rejoicing in the possibilities God has planted in my day. I am going to keep my eyes open for the happy things God has already prepared for me. I am going to open my heart to the truth that this day was made for rejoicing. I want to be good at joy. Happy God Day!

What are you celebrating today?

GOD'S YELLOW LIGHT

Sitting in a Bible study the other day, a grandmother shared a story about her five-year-old granddaughter. Her granddaughter lives out-of-town and loves to visit her grandmother and go to church with her.

The first time she visited her grandmother's church building, she stood in the doorway amazed. Near the ceiling in the room where they worship is a small stained glass window. Light was pouring through the window and the little girl was enchanted by what she saw. She told her grandmother that they had to sit in God's yellow light – the light streaming through the stained glass window. She settled into the pew, bathed in God's yellow light, and worshipped with all of her heart.

The next visit brought a new insistence. As it grew closer and closer to the time for worship, the little girl kept her eyes on the window. She was determined to once again sit in God's yellow light. It required moving from their regular seat, but the little girl once again found joy in her determination to be immersed in His light.

Now, whenever the little girl comes for a visit, they have to sit in God's yellow light. It doesn't matter where the light falls, they move to that spot and anchor themselves in the light.

What a lesson for us! I love the fact that she spotted God's yellow light. Her five-year-old faith drew her to plant her heart in its warmth. There is nowhere else she would rather be than in the light of God's love. She is willing to move outside of her comfort zone in order to stay in the light. The light guides her to where she sits, where she has her focus, and where she finds delight.

My Jesus Resolution today is to sit in God's yellow light. I want to keep my eyes open for where He is shining and join Him there. I want to be willing to move if that is what it takes to be bathed in His presence. I long for His light to define me, guide me, and illuminate every part of me.

How will His light define where you sit today?

GOD'S GPS

Flying at thirty-two thousand feet, we were all settling in for the trip to Houston. I pulled out my iPod and my book, and tried to get comfortable (or as comfortable as you can get squished together in a plane). I had just turned the page when the pilot's voice boomed over the speakers. "Ladies and Gentlemen, our navigation system has failed. We must return to the airport immediately."

The buzz in the plane started before the pilot clicked off the communication system. People all over this very full flight began wondering and worrying about what would happen next. In the end, everything was fine. We flew back to the airport (with several people anxiously watching out the window to make sure we hit the runway), the mechanics fixed the plane, and finally, several hours late, we landed in Houston.

Navigation systems are important. No one on the plane doubted the necessity of fixing the broken system. Without a navigational system, we would fly off course and crash.

Buckled into my seat, I thought about how many people try to live life without a spiritual navigational system. Despite understanding the importance of it in the physical world, how many times do I try to go my own direction, plan my own path, and plot my own course?

God gives us a GPS – Jesus. He is the Way. Walking with Him will get us exactly where we need to go. He will always lead us in the proper direction. He will choose the right path, take the right road, and open the right doors. He will get us home.

My Jesus Resolution today is to pay attention to my GPS – Jesus. I am going to focus on the directions He is giving me. I am going to check my route against the path He calls me to follow. I am going to match my footsteps with His, while trying to walk as He did. I am going to let my desire to go home pull me closer to His side.

How will you let Jesus be your GPS today?

LITTLE HANDS

His little hand reached up to grab mine. It was a simple move, a natural move. He saw me across the playground. His teacher held him back until I could reach the gate, but as soon as I was close enough, he ran to me and took my hand.

There is something extraordinary about holding hands with a child. When a child holds your hand, they literally put themselves in your shadow. They try to match your footsteps. They touch your heart while reaching for your fingers. They announce to the world where they belong.

It was an ordinary day, a part of our regular routine, but his little hand painted a picture for my soul today. With every squeeze of his fingers, I felt the hand of God. With every tug on my arm, I learned another lesson about holding on to Jesus.

When a child holds your hand, they are making a declaration of deep trust. They don't know where they are going, but they follow. They don't see the road hazards or traffic dangers, but they stay close to your side, trusting you will keep them safe. They don't set the pace, but they enjoy the time together.

Holding hands announces to the world that you belong together. You don't hold hands with strangers. Reaching for my hand is a practiced move for this little one. We fit together because our hearts are connected.

Clasping your hands together creates a place of safety. You no longer stand alone. You move with someone by your side. There is a peace that flows from knowing that you are enfolded, not only in the grasp, but in the love of someone committed to watching out for you.

My Jesus Resolution today is to be aware of my hands. I want to be like my little friend. I want to hold hands with Jesus. Who will you reach out for today?

What can holding hands with a child teach you about walking with Jesus?

LAUGHTER FROM THE FAMILY ROOM

Laughter is coming from my family room. Kids are giggling, sharing secrets, and being silly. The dog is barking at the commotion that fills the room. It is the sound of our family being together. I love it.

Our daughter will head back to school soon. I am going to miss the laughter in the family room. We will still have fun, but the melody of voices will be different without her here. She brings her own unique note to the symphony that is our family.

I wonder if God smiles when He hears laughter coming from His family. I imagine that He delights in the sounds of lives being shared, tears being cried, joys being celebrated, hugs being given, and encouragement being embraced. Each one of His children brings a different note to the chorus of praise that rises into His throne room. He knows each one of our voices. He recognizes each face. Each heart is precious to Him. There is an empty space in the family room when one of us isn't there.

You may feel lost in the crowd. You might assume that no one notices whether you are there or not. Perhaps you think that you don't make a difference. You do. God sees. He looks for your heart. He longs for you to come into the living room with His family. Without you, we are a note short.

My Jesus Resolution today is to laugh in the family room. I am not going to sit on the sidelines and just listen. I am going to link arms with God's family and sing, pray, listen, celebrate, cry, and giggle. I am going to trust that God hears my note, and cherishes the times when we all laugh together. He loves it when His family is all together. Do you want to laugh with me?

Laugh with someone in God's family today.

28

ISLAND OF LIGHT

The darkness snuck across the sky, pulling the black blanket of night over us. There was a beautiful moment when the sunset flared across the horizon line and then sunk beyond view. Looking from an airline seat, I watched God prepare our part of the earth for rest.

I sat fascinated by the inky darkness that pooled outside of my window. There were no shadows, no shapes outlined in the distance, no sense of direction. If I hadn't been able to hear the plane's engines, I would have been sure that we were suspended in ebony, not moving forward or backward.

Peering into the night, I noticed a faint smudge of color far off on the ground. It took me by surprise. For several minutes, I had been unable to see anything, detect any movement, or see beyond my reflection in the small pane of glass. The color on the ground became brighter and more distinct – an island of light in a sea of darkness. The lights of a town pushed back the inky black of night. With the light came orientation, a sense of peace, and illumination.

"You are the light of the world. A city set on a hill cannot be hidden. Nor do people light a lamp and put it under a basket, but on a stand, and it gives light to all in the house. In the same way, let your light shine before others, so that they may see your good works and give glory to your Father who is in heaven."
—Matthew 5:14-16

Our world is blanketed in darkness. Not the darkness of rest, but the suffocating blackness of sin, guilt, shame, and rebellion. Disoriented, desperate, and disillusioned, our neighbors, friends, coworkers, and loved ones watch the horizon, looking for hope and direction.

My Jesus Resolution today is to shine. I am an island of light. A child of grace, born of water and the Spirit, God fills me with Himself in order that I might illuminate the night, push back the shadows with His light, and point the way to Him. Today I am going to shine with His salvation, glow with His goodness, and light the way with His love.

How will you shine for Jesus today?

My daughter will soon be celebrating her birthday. She is a joy. Her smile lights up the room. Her laugh is a melody all its own. Her presence in our lives has been a constant source of wonder and a tool God has used to open our eyes to His nearness.

Soon we will celebrate. Cake, balloons, presents, and party signs will decorate the house. Giggling will bounce off the walls. Pictures will be taken, candles blown out, and blessings extended. Her birthday is a special day, but the day before is a day I cherish in the quiet place of my heart.

The day before my daughter was born was a day of anticipation. The reality of her presence was evident. The date and time of her arrival had been set. But she wasn't here. I knew that tomorrow everything would look different. My heart would have a different shape. My eyes would see in a new light. My hands would hold blessings destined to transform me. I waited, wondered, hoped, and prayed. I set my eyes on how God was preparing to move. I let hope shape how I walked through the moments.

We live in the day of anticipation. The reality of God's promises are evident, sure, and certain. God's faithfulness trumpets the truth that the day and hour of His arrival are set. We don't know when, but we know He is coming. We also know that when that day arrives, everything will be different. We will see with new eyes as we behold His face. We will sing with new voices, worship with new intensity, and experience joy in new and profound ways.

My Jesus Resolution today is to anticipate His coming. I am going to let the promise of His presence open my eyes. I am going to hold on to the truth that it will be soon. I am going to let the anticipation of how He is going to bless tomorrow color and shape today. Just like I did all those years ago, I am going to spend today getting ready, making sure everything is in place, and smiling about tomorrow.

Read John 14:1–3.
How will you live in
anticipation today?

SOAP

Our lives are filled with so many simple blessings. So many things that I take for granted, walk past, and overlook every day. Today I am thankful for soap. How much soap do you have in your house? I have soap in five different rooms in my house. I refill the bottles, open up new bars, and pour it into the washing machine. Such a simple blessing, and one that I take for granted too often. Soap is magical. It is wonderful. It makes bubbles. It glistens in the light. It smells good. It comes in different colors, and there are bottles to fit everyone's fancy. Soap makes us clean. This is the real beauty of soap. How many times a day do you stop and wash your hands? We don't often think about the soap that we use multiple times a day to wash the messes off our hands. It is only when there is no soap that we stop and notice. Without soap, our lives would be sticky, oily, grimy, and stinky. I am thankful for soap.

There is a cleansing agent in my life more powerful than soap. The blood of Jesus takes the deepest, darkest stains of sin and washes them away until I am whiter than snow. His blood removes my sticky selfishness, the oily presence of pride, the grimy gunk of guilt, and the stinky stench of shame. Because of the everlasting love of God, this "soap" runs freely though my life. God is never stingy with His grace. His mercies are new every morning. His forgiveness is better than those scrubbing bubbles you see in the commercials. It reaches deep, providing peace, renewal, freedom, and joy.

My Jesus Resolution is to spend today being amazed by grace. I am going to let soap be my reminder of God's presence and mercy. Every time I wash my hands, put clothes in the washing machine, load the dishwasher, and rinse the dishes, I am going to let my mind dwell on the power of God's forgiveness. I am going to notice the bubbles and stand in awe of the beauty of grace. I will look at the barcode on the bottle and be humbled by the cost that was paid to make me clean.

Thank God for His grace every time you use soap today.

My son had two teeth pulled today, involving Novocain®, gauze packs, drooling, and the whole nine yards. He was a good sport about the whole thing. It was not his favorite way to spend a day out of school, but the dentist told him that it was necessary to get those teeth out. A little pain today might save years of problems later.

God used the time in the dentist's office to remind me of an important lesson. Sometimes, the healthiest thing for us is to endure an extraction. It is necessary for things that are not good for us to be removed from our hearts. Pride, selfishness, bad habits, wrong motives, and misdirected thinking all need to be pried from our souls at the earliest possible moment. It may not seem like much, but pulling them today prevents them from growing stronger and deeper in us. A little discomfort today might save years of struggle with sin down the road.

Colossians 3:5-10 has a whole list of items that need to be extracted from our lives. God wants us to put to death (which is really what pulling teeth is all about) things like immorality, evil desires, greed, anger, filthy language, and lying. God wants to pull those things out of our lives, creating room for His image to take shape in our hearts.

My Jesus Resolution today is to settle into the Great Physician's chair, and let Him extract whatever is getting in the way of my growth. I want to be spiritually healthy. I want to grow in just the way He wants me to grow. I want to make room for the image of Jesus to take full form in my life. Even if it means pulling a couple of teeth.

Read Colossians 3:5-10.
Ask God to show you what needs to be pulled from your life so the likeness of Jesus can more fully take shape in you.

FOLLOW

I was in a strange city. The skyline broke the horizon in unfamiliar ways. As the sun warmed the clouds and painted the streets in golden light, I clutched the directions in my hand and read them again. The instructions were clear. There were turns to make, landmarks to watch for, and stop signs to notice. The address of my destination was emblazoned across the top of the map. I checked my watch. I wanted to be on time. I glanced at the directions one more time, looked out my window, and breathed a sigh of relief. I laid my map aside, buckled my seatbelt, and started my car. My friend had arrived. I followed her.

My journey took on an entirely different feel than I had anticipated. Rather than tensely gripping the wheel with one hand and the map with the other, I settled back and enjoyed the ride. I kept my eyes on my friend. When she turned, I turned. When she stopped, I stopped. I didn't try to go ahead of her. I kept my car close to her car. We went a back route to avoid some traffic, and I saw a house that made me smile. When we arrived at our destination, we were in exactly the right place at the right time.

"Follow Me" is the great invitation of the Gospels. Twenty-two times, Jesus invites us to follow Him and walk beside Him.

Following Jesus is the essence of the Christian walk. As we follow Him, we allow Him to guide us and lead us through life. He does more than show us the way. He is the Way. Following Him means we do not have to rely on our own ingenuity, resourcefulness, or directional savvy to get us to heaven. He takes us with Him. He walks beside us. He creates the path and opens the way into the presence of the Father through His own body. He calls us to stay close to His side and imitate Him.

My Jesus Resolution today is to follow Jesus. I am going to let Him take the lead. I am going to settle in by His side and enjoy the journey. I am not going to rush ahead, or try to find my own way. I am going to follow today, and wherever we go, the best part will be being together.

If you have a chance today, play Follow the Leader with a child. See what lessons you learn about following Jesus.

Excerpt from
Women Opening the Word
ABCs of a Godly Heart

GOD'S TIMING

It was a three-state weekend. I still marvel that I can get on an airplane and be in an entirely different part of the country in only a few hours. This weekend was full of blessings, but the weather stood out as one of the big signposts that pointed me to the heart of God.

In south Texas, where I live, spring was in full bloom. Grass was growing, trees were budding out, flowers were beginning to show their beauty, temperatures had warmed up, and yellow pine pollen blanketed everything.

I flew to eastern Tennessee where spring was just beginning to show its promise. The ground was not yet green, but yellow daffodils poked their heads out of the earth. The sky was a freshly washed blue, bringing with it the hint that spring was on its way. The trees had no leaves, but the warming temperatures offered an incentive for them to pop out of their winter rest.

From Tennessee, I made a stop in Chicago. This weekend, Chicago was blanketed in a sparkling garment of snow. The freezing temperatures ensured that the newly fallen snow would stick around for a while. Coats were still the order of the day.

In the midst of these different scenes, I saw a lesson about God's timing. He works in each of us within the timing that is best for where we are in life. God doesn't bring spring to the entire country all in one day. It blossoms in our land, just like it moves in our lives. We may look at the way God is moving in someone else, wishing that His timing worked the same way in our lives. But His timing is just like the coming of spring – perfect for where we are, and what He wants to bring to life in our hearts.

My Jesus Resolution today is to be satisfied in God's timing. I am going to trust that He is going to move in me at just the right moment. I am going to look for the signs of His coming. I am going to rejoice in the evidence of His movement. I am going to find peace in the fact that God is never too slow or too fast – He is perfect in everything He does. I am going to let His springtime bloom inside of me, and pray that it is a signpost that points others to Him.

Where today do you need to rest in God's perfect timing?

HANDMADE GIFTS

The most special gifts I have received have come from the hands of my children. I have a gingham pillow cross-stitched with "MOM" made by my daughter in fifth grade. One of my sons put popsicle sticks together and made a cross. It sits prominently in my kitchen. Another son drew a picture that captures our family through his eyes. They are special to me, not because they are great masterpieces or magnificent works of art. They are treasured because my children made them just for me.

Handmade gifts are special. Each one represents an investment of love, time, energy, and thought that went into its making. When you hold a homemade gift, you know that you were on someone's mind, in their heart, and the focus of their hands.

God loves to give handmade gifts. You are His treasure and His delight. He has touched today, filling it with markers, blessings, and people that are all meant to stand as reminders in your day of how much He loves you. The bird you hear is singing a love song. The flowers along the way were sent just for you. The smile you see on someone's face is a reflection of the delight God has just for you. Blue skies, tall trees, and tiny ladybugs all proclaim the immensity of His love. Each one is a handmade gift meant to draw your eyes to His heart.

The cross frames God's greatest gift. It is the place where love intertwines with surrender, holiness is called to bear the weight of sin, and two beams and three nails reveal how far God is willing to go to pursue you. Nothing but the hands of God Himself could create such a precious gift.

My Jesus Resolution today is to have eyes open to see the gifts God has planted in my day. They are there. Hand-created reminders that I am on His mind, in His heart, and the focus of His passion. I want to keep a count of all the ways I see God reminding me of His love today. I am going to experience the delight of being extravagantly loved.

Pay attention to the handmade gifts God gives you today. Thank Him for having His hands so completely on your day.

A NEW BIBLE

I got a new Bible yesterday. It was time. Pages were falling out, the binding was breaking, pieces of Scripture were sliding out of place. Still, getting a new Bible fills me with mixed emotions.

My old Bible is like an old friend. Its pages fall open and reveal truths learned, tears cried, faith built up, pride broken, prayers offered, insights gleaned, humility discovered, healing bestowed, and worship lifted up. Holding it close to my heart, I reflect on the journey we have taken together. My old Bible has been my companion, my champion, my comfort, my mirror, and my challenger. In its pages, I have met God and been changed. Through its words, I have heard the voice of the Lord. In every verse and chapter, I have been given a picture of Jesus that has captivated my heart.

I am excited about my new Bible. Its crisp pages hold the promise of adventures to be taken, lessons to be learned, praises to be sung, sacrifices to be given, faith to be strengthened, and surrender to be offered. In its new pages, I will meet the God who I already know. He will use the words to teach me more about His heart, to call me deeper into His will, and to challenge me to give myself more completely to Him.

The same truth rests in both books. The worn, crumpled pages testify to the journey I have already taken. The fresh, new pages lay out a road map for my heart to travel in the days ahead. Living and active, the words will call to my soul. In them, I will hear anew the invitation of Jesus as He says, "Follow Me." My old Bible taught me many ways to answer His call. My new Bible will continue to guide me on the path to looking like Jesus.

My Jesus Resolution today is to make my new Bible my old friend. I am going to welcome it into my life like the companion God means for it to be. I want its words to resonate in my heart, to be lived out in my life, and to shape me into the image of the Son. I am going to take it with me on the road, in my house, in the car, and through my day. Someday soon, I won't notice the stiffness of the binding or the crispness of the pages. All I will hear is His voice and all I will see is the face of Jesus.

In what way is your Bible like an old friend?

FLOWERS

I love flowers. It really doesn't matter what kind – just flowers. Fields of them. Bouquets of them. Gardens brimming with them. Pots overflowing with them. I love flowers. I delight in the myriad of colors and the variety of shapes. I enjoy the aromas and the delicate details. They are touches of exquisite beauty that God created for our joy and wonder.

This past weekend, someone gave me a packet of flower seeds. "Plant these right now," she said. "It's the right time." The picture on the envelope looks great. I know – the seeds are still sitting on my desk.

I love flowers, but I don't want to plant the seeds. It's too much work. It takes too much time. Not to mention that pesky dirt messing up my manicure. How many opportunities for beauty do I miss because I don't plant the seeds?

My Jesus Resolution today is to plant some seeds – seeds of kindness, encouragement, friendship, and joy. I am going to invest myself in cultivating peace, quietness, and praise in the garden of my soul. I want to plant some gratitude and laughter in my family. I am going to find a friend and express appreciation. Planting seeds is a matter of being deliberate about beauty. Seeds take time to grow, but the results will take your breath away.

What seeds will you plant today?

I am going to go apply for a passport. There is a possibility of travel in my future and I want to be ready. Getting a passport is a process. There are pictures to be taken, forms to be filled out, lines to stand in, and fees to be paid. Passports require effort, but when you hold one, it opens the door to adventure and new experiences.

Traveling in another land is exciting. It opens your eyes to the world in ways that stretch your imagination and understanding. You get to try new foods, hear new languages, walk in new paths, and experience the world in a new context. It should help us count our blessings, stand in awe of God's vast power, and see the cross with new eyes.

Standing in another land also underscores the truth that you are not at home. All of the textures, flavors, aromas, and sounds of a different place and culture help you see home differently. What we once took for granted becomes the familiar for which we long. As much as we drink in the beauty of a foreign country, we thirst for home.

Passports do more than let you into another country. They identify your citizenship. They declare where you belong. They mark you as a resident of a land. Those little books are your lifeline to home. They provide proof of your rights and carry with them responsibilities.

In one sense, the Holy Spirit is our passport. He seals us as God's children. He identifies our citizenship. He marks us as belonging to heaven. Traveling in this world, He helps us to see God's hand all around us and to appreciate the beauty and diversity that make up this grand globe, drawing our hearts to the cross with each step. He also reminds us that this is not home. Our citizenship is somewhere else.

He prods us to not get too comfortable or plant our roots too deeply in the temporary. He is our lifeline to the Father, and helps us remember where we truly belong.

My Jesus Resolution today is to celebrate my citizenship. I am going to walk through this world today – wherever I may be – aware of where I truly belong. I want to invest in the joy of experiencing all the beauty of this life while keeping my eyes on the ways God is pulling my heart toward home. And everywhere I travel today, I am going to hold on to my passport.

What are you most looking forward to about heaven?

The Jesus Resolution
I LOVE YOU BIGGER

...that you, being rooted and grounded in love, may have strength to comprehend with all the saints what is the breadth and length and height and depth, and to know the love of Christ that surpasses knowledge, that you may be filled with all the fullness of God.
—Ephesians 3:17b-19

My son and I used to play a silly game when he was little. It was the "I love you bigger" game. One of us would say, "I love you," the other would respond with "I love you bigger," and it would skyrocket from there. "I love you wider." "I love you deeper." "I love you taller." "I love you to China." "I love you more than all the stars in the sky." "I love you more than all the drops of water in the ocean."

One day, when my son could think of nothing else to say, he said, "I love you more than God and Jesus." He got an incredible grin on his face because he knew that there was nothing that could top that. It was a neat moment because he caught a glimpse of the immensity of God's love. It was a teachable moment because we got to talk about the truth that nobody loves us more than God and Jesus.

My Jesus Resolution today is to catch a glimpse of God's love. Paul's prayer for the Ephesians is my prayer for my heart today. I am going to talk to God about how much I love Him. I want to watch His face and experience His delight when He points to the cross and says, "I love you bigger."

Read Romans 8:38-39 to catch a glimpse of God's great love for you.

47

SCANS

Another trip through the airport. I do a lot of traveling so I am pretty familiar with the security routines. Bags get x-rayed, shoes come off, and liquids are put in little bags. I travel enough that I can move into the "experienced travelers" line at the airport. It is routine. I know the drill. I have my boarding pass and identification ready, and work to be patient while the security people explain to the man in front of me why he can't bring his lighter and knife on the plane.

Now there is a new step in the security process. Body scans. Regardless of how you view this next wave in security technology, the threat of terrorism now has a very personal impact on the way we move through our world. Stepping into the machine allows safety officials to check for danger concealed from sight.

As I went through the security process this time, I wondered what would happen if there was a machine that could scan our hearts as easily as it scans our bodies. What if all the things hidden in my heart where displayed on a screen? What would others see?

While not minimizing the dangers inherent in weapons and explosives, the most dangerous things are often carried in our hearts. Pride, selfishness, greed, bitterness, and fear are profoundly destructive. They eat away at our souls, poisoning not only our own lives, but the spirits of those around us.

> *"For the LORD sees not as man sees: man looks on the outward appearance, but the LORD looks on the heart."* — **1 Samuel 16:7b**

God looks at our hearts every day. He keeps His eye on us in order to turn us away from danger and to guide us into His arms. He longs to see His Word written on our hearts. He fills our days with His presence so we will bow our hearts before His glory. He wants surrender and sacrifice to shape our souls. When He looks at our hearts, He wants to see Jesus.

My Jesus Resolution today is to do a heart scan. I am going to examine the motives that drive me and the priorities that determine my direction. I want to pull out what I treasure and see what it says about my heart. I am going to ask God to do a thorough search and remove anything destructive and dangerous. I am going to let David's cry in Psalm 51:10 be the theme of my day. *"Create in me a clean heart, O God."*

Read Psalm 139:23-24.
Ask God to search and
cleanse your heart.

MESSY WITH JESUS

My daughter went back to school. She was home from college, and it was a joy. She will settle back into her routine with friends, classes, homework, and papers, and do great. The rest of us will jump into our schedules and miss her like crazy.

What I am noticing now that she's gone is that my house is clean. Too clean. When she is home, you know it. There are shoes, jackets, purses, books, and "girl stuff" everywhere. (Did I mention shoes?) I stand in the house, look around, and know she's home. The evidence of her presence is everywhere. There are chick flicks stacked next to a spot that is usually only visited by aliens and superheroes. I can tell when she has walked through a room because there is the hint of a different perfume in the air. The table has its extra chair back. We have to make room in the bathroom. Someone has to sit in the backseat of the van.

There was a time when the mess would have bothered me. Not today. Today she has helped me see God. I want my life to be messy with Jesus. I long to look around and know that He is at home in my heart. That He has changed what I watch, filled in the empty spaces, and challenged me to rearrange my life to make more room for Him, to humble myself so He can sit in the driver's seat, and to smell the aroma of Christ on the air and know that He is walking with me into each room of my life.

My Jesus Resolution today calls me to be messy. I want to be so filled with Jesus that others can't help but notice His presence in my life. I want the floor of my heart to be covered with His words, my mind to be filled with His thoughts, and my soul to be flooded with His praise. Want to be messy with me?

Where can others most clearly see Jesus in you?

BLUEBONNETS

There was a riot of colors splattered across the landscape of the Texas hill country this weekend. The entire palette of the rainbow was painted in bold strokes across the fields, on the hills, and over the countryside. Bright yellows splashed down next to pockets of pale pink. Purple and scarlet competed against orange and white. Flowers carpeted the roadways and covered the meadows. Streaks of color danced in the grasses as if God took a paintbrush, spun around, and let the hues fall where they may.

The bluebonnets, however, were the best. The entire bouquet of yellows, scarlets, purples, reds, and pinks served as a frame for the bluebonnets. Bluebonnets are the color of the sky right before dawn – a deep blue with a white top. Examining a single bluebonnet reveals profound beauty. The intricacy and delicate detail speak to the glory of God.

It is in seeing fields of bluebonnets, however, that you catch their real beauty. Clustered together, they take your breath away. Just like Christians.

Each individual Christian is a remarkable testimony to the beauty of grace. The transformation of a single soul is a miracle worth celebrating. The details of Christ seen in a life devoted to Him speak to the glory of God.

When Christians stand together, linked in heart and purpose to Jesus, there is a radical beauty that God uses to take the world's breath away. Clusters of bluebonnets along the road remind me of congregations of Christians committed to planting God's glory in their own little piece of the world. Some are big, while others are small – each settling into the soil and planting a testimony to the grace of our Lord.

Then I turned the corner, and got a picture of heaven. On a back country road, I saw a field entirely enveloped in bluebonnets. Millions of them, covering the ground as far as the eye could see. Words are inadequate to describe the beauty of that field. They fall short, and I am thankful for that. I like the idea that there are no words to describe exactly what heaven will be like. We will have to see it to understand it and appreciate it.

My Jesus Resolution today is to imitate the bluebonnets. I am going to bloom where I am. I am going to plant myself in the midst of a group of hearts that are committed to looking like Jesus. Linked together, we give the world a glimpse of God's glory. I want my life to testify to the beauty of His grace and the wonder of His love. He takes my breath away. Let's stand together today and give the world a reason to pause.

Who can you encourage to bloom where they are today?

SET FREE

You are deeply loved. God's passion for you spills over into every part of your day. The blessings you enjoy are evidence of His care. His power raises the sun, paints the flowers, and puts sparkle into the stars – just for you. He has seen you at your best, and at your worst. He loves you. He knows what you look like in the morning. He sees you doing laundry, cooking dinner, driving your car, and checking your mail. He loves you through all of it. He sees the deep wounds sin leaves on your heart. He aches as He watches the chains of slavery wrap tighter around your soul. He still loves you. He loves you when you walk away from Him. He loves you when you run toward His open arms.

He loves you so much. The cross stands as proof of His love. He saw your chains, checked His heart, and made His way toward your Egypt. He fought the dragon, endured the thorns, and spent three nights in a tomb in order to set you free. He loves you. He has been pursuing you your entire life. He calls your name. He holds out His hand. He brushes your cheek with the wind. His dream, His purpose, and His plan all center on bringing you home. He loves you, and He longs to see you free indeed.

> *"So if the Son sets you free, you will be free indeed."* — **John 8:36**

This is the life He created you to share with Him. This is the intense desire of His heart. You are the reason He made the journey, endured the thorns, and fought the dragon. Being free indeed means saying "Yes" to Jesus. Every minute. Every day. For the rest of your life.

My Jesus Resolution today is to say "yes" to the set free life Jesus has in mind for me. Being free indeed is, in its essence, the freedom to choose Jesus. Every day you get to choose who you are going to follow. Every day you get to pick where to set your focus. Every day you get to decide which vision you are going to let define your life. Being free indeed is the everyday choice to see Jesus, follow Jesus, imitate Jesus, love Jesus, praise Jesus, bow before Jesus, surrender to Jesus, listen to Jesus, be transformed by Jesus, and walk like Jesus.

*Read John 8:31–36.
In what way has Jesus
set you free?*

**Excerpt from
Women Opening the Word
Set Free**

He took the stage with a flourish. It was my son's first time to be in character. He tried out for a one act play at school and was blessed to become a part of the cast. They memorized lines, practiced their parts, and rehearsed the play for weeks. Costumes were prepared, stage directions were given, and even make-up was applied to make the character come to life.

He did great. The play was a success, delighting an audience of parents and friends assembled to cheer them on in the school auditorium.

At the end of the play festival, my son received some direction and advice from a seasoned professional. It was neat to hear the gentleman point out the things my son had done well and outline small steps he could take to improve his performance. The piece of advice that drew my attention was simple – commit to the character. When on stage, completely become the character. Talk like him, react like him, move like him. Don't do anything outside of the character that you want to become.

Interesting advice. His words hold encouragement beyond teaching a student how to act in a play. Shakespeare is the one who said that "all the world's a stage." We live our lives before an audience. Each person we meet watches us to see if we are living in character – if we are committed to living out the character of Jesus.

Of course, we don't put on a costume and pretend to be Jesus. Rather, we long to actually experience a transformation that changes our character to look like His. We want to show the world a reflection of Christ. We long to imitate the way He moves, talks, acts, and relates to others. In order to do that, we have to commit to living out His character in each moment of our lives.

My Jesus Resolution today is to commit my heart to being His, reflecting Christ in all I do and say. I want others to see a clear picture of Jesus in me. All the world is a stage. My neighbors, family, and friends are watching, looking for Him in my actions and words. Today, I am going to commit to His character, trusting that when I hide myself in Him, He will be in the spotlight.

How will you commit yourself to living in the character of Jesus today?

I am not very patient. Today I was standing in line at the store waiting for customer service. It didn't take long for me to check the time and start tapping my toe. We tend to view waiting as a waste. We see it as down time that isn't being used in the most efficient way. Waiting holds little value in our society because it is deemed unproductive. It doesn't move us forward on the ladder to success, buy us the newest gadget, or contribute to reaching a higher status. In fact, the longer you have to wait in our society, the more of a nobody the world says you really are.

What if I could view my waiting times differently? What if I could see them as God-given moments to touch the circumstance in which I find myself waiting with His power and grace? When I am standing in line, holding on the phone, waiting for my email to download, standing at the bus stop, or waiting for a friend to arrive, I have two choices. My first, and usual, choice is to view those minutes as delays in getting to where I want to go and what I hope to accomplish. Seeing them this way makes me impatient and irritable. The world needs to run on my schedule. It moves me to the center, allowing me to demand that everything run at my pace.

The second option is to fill those waiting moments with God. I could spend my time in line at the store praying for the people in the line with me, the clerk who is working hard to help us, and the blessings of being able to buy what I need. Waiting time could be watching time – watching for God to move, searching for His fingerprints, or soaking in the beauty He plants all around us. At the bus stop, I can pray for my children. In the parking lot, I can ask God to be in the middle of the conversation I will have with my friend. Waiting times can be times of blessing rather than a burden or a bother, if we infuse them with Him.

My Jesus Resolution today is to wait with joy. I will see every line I wait in today as a place to meet God. I will ask the Lord how I can be a blessing to those waiting with me. I resolve to wait with expectation, anticipating that God will cause those minutes to overflow with His presence. I am going to use these waiting minutes to make my heart tender to the truth that God continually waits for me.

Will you commit to waiting with joy today?

I KNOW HE CAN

My grandmother used to tell me the story of "The Little Engine That Could." Do you remember it? A little train, the smallest train of all, faced big obstacles and overwhelming odds. There were people to carry, goods to deliver, mountains to climb, and barriers that the Little Engine had to overcome. He met each challenge with a positive attitude, telling himself over and over again, "I think I can. I think I can. I think I can." My grandmother's voice would take on a train engine quality as she described him puffing up the tall mountain. I held my breath and hoped that the Little Engine would make it. And he did. I can remember the smile that washed over my grandmother's face as the train pulled into the station and she tucked me into bed.

We still run on an "I think I can" track. Our world tells us that every problem we face should be met with an "I think I can" attitude and all will be well. The trouble is it's not true, and deep down we know it. There are things we can't fix, mountains that really are too tall to climb, and situations so bleak and dark that no amount of positive attitude will turn it around.

Christians move through life proclaiming something different – "I know He can. I know He can. I know He can." Our strength to face the mountains isn't found in ourselves, but in the power of our God. The broken things in our lives can be mended by the One who holds the universe together. Our confidence rests not in the stock market, the government, or our own can-do attitude, but in the unwavering, overwhelming grace of our Lord.

My Jesus Resolution today is to repeat "I know He can" throughout the day. A moment of joy, a time of sorrow, a high mountain, a deep valley, and ordinary steps will all find me depending on the strength of my God. I don't have to do it by myself. I can't do it by myself. God reminds me that I can ride on His shoulders and let Him pull the load. I am going to say it over and over today. He is very close and He can.

Do you more often run with an "I think I can" attitude or an "I know He can" perspective?

CARS

It was a playing day. A little friend spread his smiles among the members of my family. We played ball, shot baskets, had races, tickled, hugged, and laughed. In the midst of the fun, my son suddenly got a smile on his face and ran upstairs. He came back with a plastic box filled with little cars.

The cars are treasures from years ago. Tucked in the back of his closet, he saw them through the eyes of our little friend. He handed the box to his buddy and waited with anticipation. The reaction was worth the wait.

"WOW!" echoed across the room. Excitement erupted and laughter bubbled over. A whole tub of cars provided enough smiles to fill many hours.

Wonder kept him glued to the box. Each car was worthy of an exclamation of delight. My kids were bored with the cars after a few minutes. They looked at the wheels and shiny colors and shrugged their shoulders. Not our little friend. He examined each one with great care. "Awesome!" "Cool!" and "Look at this!" rang out as he demanded our attention. Where our eyes glazed over at the sight of so many cars, he found joy in the details.

God is more like our friend than me. God never tires of delighting in the personal details of each individual. Our eyes may not notice, but His heart never stops exclaiming over the ones He loves. Too often, I stop looking at faces and just see masses of people. I miss the beauty, the unique ways God is working in each life, and the preciousness of each soul. God never does. He holds each one in His hand and smiles.

My Jesus Resolution today is to look at others the way God looks at me. I want to see the value in each soul. I want to find the beauty in each heart. I want to notice the way God is working in each life. I want to see Jesus in the faces of those He loved enough to die for. I want to extend grace to those on the journey. I want to smile and share God's delight in discovering the uniqueness He has planted in each person.

Start today by looking in the mirror and paying attention to what God celebrates in you.

NAPS

I will admit that I love napping. There is something soothing about curling up under a blanket and taking a few minutes to rest in the middle of the day. Unfortunately, I don't get to take very many naps, but the idea of a nap always sounds good.

Sleep doesn't seem like a very spiritual topic, but it is a gift from God. He designed our bodies to sleep. He introduced the rhythm of rest into our world from the very beginning. The cycle of evening and morning were celebrated at creation.

It is interesting how much our society resists sleep. We stay up later, get up earlier, and rush through our days trying to get more and more done. We think that if we can just move a little faster, stay up a little longer, or go a little further, then our world will become the ordered place we imagine that it should be. The only thing that ever really happens is that we get tired…really tired.

Sleep is necessary for our spiritual health. When we are tired, we get frantic, worried, and irritable. Our sense of God's presence wanes as our focus turns inward. Our perspective gets misaligned as our energy drains. It is difficult to pray when we are tired. Worship fades when we are weary.

Solomon reminds us of God's wisdom. *"…for he gives to his beloved sleep"* (Psalm 127:2b). Sleep is a blessing from God. It shows us His love and His care. In sleep, He refreshes us, renews us, and reenergizes us. Sleep is healing, both for the body and the spirit. When we sleep, we put ourselves in His hands, honor the rhythm He created for our bodies, and trust that He will care for us during our rest.

My Jesus Resolution today is to rest. I am going to be deliberate about stopping, putting it down, and resting quietly in His presence. I want to honor my Creator and trust that I am fearfully and wonderfully made. I am going to recognize my dependence on Him in everything, even the need for sleep. Shhh… I'm going to go take a nap.

How will you be deliberate about rest today?

Generosity is a rare gift these days. Today I am thankful for someone in my life who is exceedingly generous. She gives of herself. She opens the door to her heart and pours out the aroma of Christ on those blessed enough to meet her. In being generous, she shares what the Lord has given her with those around her.

What makes this woman's generosity so unique is not the amount that she gives. It is the way in which she gives. She gives as if it is her delight. She gives with a smile, almost as if she and God are sharing a secret. She looks for quiet ways to bless the lives of others. She searches out opportunities to enrich the hearts of those she meets. She richly blesses others with her faith and enthusiasm for what God is doing.

Some people give and want to hold it over you. They swing their generosity like a guillotine above your neck. Others use their generosity like a spotlight, highlighting their pious actions and saintly selves. There are those who give grudgingly. Others who give thoughtlessly. Many who give out of duty.

> *And God is able to make all grace abound to you, so that having all sufficiency in all things at all times, you may abound in every good work.* —2 Corinthians 9:8

What this heart of generosity has taught me is to look to the heart of Jesus. Her giving echoes the giving of Jesus. He loves to give. He gives graciously and abundantly, enriching our lives with the gifts of His presence, power, and provision. He fills our hearts to overflowing so that His grace will spill out on those around us, inviting them to dive into the ocean of His love. He gives sacrificially, opening His heart, giving His life, and pouring out His Spirit. When I learn to give generously, I learn to be more like Jesus.

My Jesus Resolution today is to be more generous. I long to be generous with my time, talents, money, faith, friendship, and joy. I want to be gracious in the way I give. I want to find the deep joy that flows from pouring myself out. I want to be sacrificial without calling attention to my sacrifice. I want to be so thankful for God's gifts to me that I can't help but generously share them with everyone I meet.

How will you be generous today?

BEAUTY IN UNEXPECTED PLACES

The other day I was taking a walk and saw an unusual sight. A flower, in full bloom, was growing in the storm drain by the side of the road. It was purple and lush green set against a backdrop of grey concrete and darkness. I did a double take. There in a place with little sunlight, prone to rushing waters during a rainstorm and dry stretches in between, was a flower. In this unlikely spot, beauty took a chance and grew.

Beauty is one of God's fingerprints. Sometimes we see beauty in grand vistas – the tall mountains, the sandy dunes, or the crystal clear waters. Sometimes beauty is hidden in unexpected places. The same is true of people's hearts. Some of the most profound beauty is found in those whose lives make growing beauty difficult. Despite our society's obsession to the contrary, true beauty is not defined by genetics, body type, or fashion magazines. Beauty is a choice. It is a move of the heart. True beauty is found in a life that has been touched by God.

Think of someone you know who is truly beautiful. You know, the kind of beauty that flows from the inside out. The color of their hair or the shape of their eyes doesn't matter nearly as much as what you see in their heart. A life that radiates the beauty of Jesus is irresistible. Seeing God in the eyes of another is stunning. When someone is full of the Spirit, it catches our breath.

My Jesus Resolution today is to keep my eyes open for true beauty. I am not going to let myself be defined by the world's standards. I am going to look for His beauty in unexpected places – a person some might overlook, a place where beauty might not be obvious, a time or circumstance that is less than ideal, even the mirror. God plants His beauty in unexpected places. Where will you see His beauty today?

Sing "Let the beauty of Jesus be seen in me" out loud today.

STOP, DROP, AND ROLL

The moment comes for us all. The doctor calls you in or the phone rings in the still of the night. The checkbook balance goes red before the bills have been paid or your child's principal asks you to come in for a conference. A moment of crisis. Need dripping fear into your heart. Spirits overwhelmed by loneliness, frustration, or exhaustion. Perhaps the moment isn't as earth-shattering but, in that moment, is equally overwhelming. The baby is sick. Your car dies in the intersection. The work project due yesterday is late. How do you react? Call a friend or drop to your knees? Grab a cup of coffee or drink from the Living Water? Complain to a colleague or quiet your soul? I fear most often during times of stress or crisis, our first reaction is to seek the solace of a friend before the comfort of God. Only later do we realize our need to bring our situation before our Heavenly Father. Oh dear friend, if we could just learn to run to Jehovah-Rapha first! While He may not choose to remove the painful situation from our lives, He does promise to heal our spirits and cover our hearts with peace.

How do we learn to run to Him first? Practice in moments not overwhelmed with stress and need. Why do we teach our children what to do in case of a fire? We teach them to stop, drop, and roll, and plan fire escape routes from our homes because we want them to know what to do when the need arises. During the emergency, it is too late. In the same way, developing a relationship with God during a time of crisis is difficult, though not impossible. How much grief we would save ourselves by knowing the heart of our God before the flames overwhelm us.

My Jesus Resolution today is to practice running to God. I am going to turn to Him for all the small emergencies that consume so much of my energy. I want to invite Him into the moments of calm and quiet. I long to see His face when I first wake up and when I close my eyes. I am going to train my heart to seek Him first, so that when a dark moment comes, I will know how to find the Light.

How will you train your heart to seek Him first today?

Excerpt from
Women Opening the Word
God, Pass By Me

WHATEVER YOU DO

I learned it in eleventh grade. My teacher made us memorize it for a test. The quote by Thomas Henry Huxley made a deep impression on me, sticking with me all these years. "Perhaps the most valuable result of all education is the ability to make yourself do the thing you have to do, when it ought to be done, whether you like it or not. It is the first lesson that ought to be learned."[1]

Sometimes we have to do things we don't like. It's just life. We wish everything could be the sweet things, the fun times, or the soaring moments, but the reality is we have to do the other stuff too. There will always be laundry to do, bills to pay, messes to clean up, and not so pleasant tasks to get through. Huxley's quote gives us a "just get in there and get it done" tool that is valuable. Sometimes, you just have to take a deep breath, roll up your sleeves, and get through it.

Paul, however, gives us a context for all of our tasks – the tough ones and the easy ones. *Whatever you do, work heartily, as for the Lord and not for men"* (Colossians 3:23). Everything we do can be an act of worship. Every task can be a moment offered to the Lord. It doesn't matter what it is, whether we like it or not, or if it is something noticed and valued by others. When we live with surrendered hearts, every move we make takes on eternal significance. Our actions echo through heaven. When we offer whatever we do to the Lord, we are asking Him to infuse it with His purpose, presence, and power. The task that really isn't your favorite can become a sacrifice of praise that sings His glory when you do it for the Lord, and not for men.

My Jesus Resolution today is to look at my to-do list with Colossians 3:23 eyes. I am going to be deliberate about keeping my eyes on Jesus as I work through each task. I am going to offer each movement to the Lord as the sacrifice of a heart that is learning to reflect Him. I want to measure each moment, not by whether I like it or not, but by how pleasing it is to Him. It is possible to find joy in everything I do today, because today I am going to do everything for Him.

Where do you need to have Colossians 3:23 eyes today?

We are having fun today. A little friend has come over to play. He makes us laugh while we sing, growl like lions, hunt for dinosaurs, and play trains. In loving him, we have been impressed again with the profound truths learned at the feet of a little child.

Several times already this afternoon, our preschool friend has said, "Let me tell you a story…." Each time he does, we grin. We love his imagination. We delight in the way he tells us what is on his mind. We smile at how our hearts are interconnected. But we grin because he sounds just like his daddy.

Children are amazing recorders of the way we act and speak. It doesn't take long to discover our attitudes, priorities, and sense of God echoing in the voices of the little ones who share our lives. They teach us that our words and actions have an impact far deeper than we might have imagined. They help us see the world through new eyes as we reexamine what our choices might look like from their perspective.

Our little friend's penchant for storytelling also reminds us of something else. We want the Father to be recognizable in our words. We want the echo of His voice to be heard in everything we say. We are called to imitate the One who loves us beyond measure, wraps us in His arms, and claims us as His own.

My Jesus Resolution today is to watch a child so I can learn how to be His child. I want to hold hands, forgive with ease, love with abandon, play with joy, and let the time with my Father soak deeply into every part of who I am. I want the family resemblance to be marked and noticeable. I want others to grin when they hear me say something that sounds exactly like something my Abba would say.

In what way do you most resemble your Father?

HE'S MINE

Every summer, we take a group of teens to do VBS for underprivileged kids. It is the neatest trip. Teens who never have to worry about going hungry, having a roof over their heads, or what they are going to wear spend a week sharing Jesus with kids who struggle with the most basic things in life. I love spending this week with them. Perspectives are altered, hearts are softened, Jesus is lifted up, and blessings previously taken for granted are appreciated.

The first and last days of our trip are always the most interesting. This year was the first year my oldest son went on the trip. Hanging around the church building with the other teens, they all slept on the pews, listened to music, or talked among themselves while waiting for the children to come. "The bus is here!" brings everyone to life. All of the sudden, swarms of little hands and feet come racing down the aisles. Squeals of delight fill the air as excitement about VBS erupts from little hearts.

I watched my son's face as he looked deeply into the eyes of children who had already seen more heartache than he had ever known. A look of surprise filled my son's expression as big eyes shining from a little face took his measure. The boy was scrawny. Small for his age, he looked hungry. Not for food, but for attention and love. He took one look at my son, attached himself to this big kid's leg, and said, "He's mine!"

That little boy didn't leave my son's side for the entire week. He stayed fastened onto that leg. Wherever my son went, the boy went. Whatever my son did, the boy did. They ate together, read the Bible together, and played together. By the end of the week, the boy had my son's hat and his heart. They both cried on our final day together.

The picture of those boys will stay forever etched in my heart. It is a picture of God captured in Kool-Aid smiles. I see God in my son. Big and strong, he embraced being embraced with a quiet passion. I see myself in the little boy. Hungry, I can run to God's side, grab on, and say with confidence, "He's mine!"

My Jesus Resolution today is to run and grab hold of God. One of the greatest promises God makes is the promise to give us His heart. He tells me that He has made the trip, opened the door, paid the price, and given His all so that I can be with Him. I can fix my heart firmly in the foundation of His faithfulness, declaring with resolution and excitement, "He's mine!" and then never leave His side.

Decide to grab hold of God today and never let go.

TO-DO LISTS

Everybody is busy. We all have full calendars, long to-do lists, and priority-filled agendas. Sometimes in the midst of all my busyness, it becomes hard to see God. The days become blurs of activity, and I miss His presence. I run, try to catch up, cross things off my list, and don't connect with the One who loves me beyond measure.

What if I could look at my to-do list differently? My to-do lists tend to be "me" focused. This is what I have to do. These are the places I have to go and the things I have to accomplish with my time and effort. What if, instead, I could see that list as a road map for spending the day with God?

Here are a few ideas that might change the way we look at our to-do lists:

- Make your to-do list a pray-do list. Use your to-do list as a prayer guide for the day. God wants to be intimately involved in each piece of your life. He wants to help you with the laundry, your work deadline, and paying the bills. He longs for you to be as aware of Him at the grocery store as you are while reading your Bible. Praying through your to-do list invites God into each movement of your day. Ask Him to bless you and walk with you as you complete each task. Ask for His wisdom as you make decisions. Open the door for God to be part of each conversation you have and present in the places you go.

- Put God on the list. Plan specific times in your day to meet God. You have other appointments on your list. Why not God? Take two or three minutes every couple of hours to be still before the Lord. Refocus your mind and your heart. Come back to center. Seek His face. He promises you will always find Him.

- Let your list be a living record. As you cross things off your to-do list, make a brief note of where you saw God in the moment. Pay attention to beauty seen, prayers answered, doors opened, wisdom bestowed, energy infused, comfort felt, resources provided, friendships deepened, and blessings received. Crossing something off the list is only half the fun. Let each part of your list become a testimony to the way you and God have walked through the day together.

My Jesus Resolution today is to look at my to-do list with new eyes. Instead of a mountain I have to climb by myself, I am going to look for all the opportunities that my list gives me to meet God. I am going to pray for the people and activities on my list, asking God to fill each part of my day. I want to meet God throughout my day, so I am going to be deliberate about turning off the noise and turning my heart to Him. I am going to keep track of the way I discover His fingerprints on my to-do list. I am going to see my to-do list as a record of God's movement in my life, rather than a speedometer of my day.

How will you let your to-do list help you meet God today?

BREATHING

I have a cold. Nothing serious or major, just several days of tissues, medicine, and misery. You know the feeling – sore throat, drippy nose, and stuffiness. Everything feels clogged. My ears feel like they have cotton stuffed into them. My voice is scratchy and running at about half volume (of course, not everyone thinks this is a bad thing). My nose is sore, and I can't breathe.

Breathing is about more than taking air into our lungs. Breathing is life – both physically and spiritually. When God created man, He fashioned legs, arms, eyes, and smiles, then He breathed the breath of life into him. This breath did more than animate the body. It gave life to the soul.

Our language reveals our understanding of how breathing is connected to life. If something amazing happens, we talk about how it takes our breath away. Spectacular beauty can cause us to catch our breath. When stress overwhelms us, we encourage someone to take a deep breath. We cry with joy when babies take their first breath. We weep when someone breathes their last.

When Jesus wanted to assure the disciples of His presence in their lives, He breathed on them. It is a moment that echoes with Eden-like significance. New life in the Spirit. Peace beyond understanding. Joy without limit.

My Jesus Resolution today is to breathe. I am going to let each breath remind me of the presence of God. I am going to remember that life flows from Him and be grateful for each breath He gives me. I want to live in such a way that I breathe love, graciousness, encouragement, and thanksgiving into the lives of those around me. Take a deep breath with me today. Fill your life with Jesus.

How will you let each breath you take today remind you of Jesus?

Invisibility seems like it would be a cool superpower. We could glide into rooms unnoticed, listen in on top-secret conversations, and find the clue that will save the world. In real life, being invisible is more a matter of the heart than a superpower. We all have an ache to be seen. This isn't a grab for personal glory or a pathological need for attention. It is a need wired into our souls – a need to be known, loved, valued, and appreciated.

Feeling invisible makes our hearts heavy. We move through our days wondering if we register in anyone's eyes as anything other than a solid object to move around. We live in such a fast-paced world that it is easy to be surrounded by people, but never connect to anyone.

Hagar knows how you feel. Mistreated, abused, ignored, used, and taken for granted, Hagar feels so invisible she flees into the desert. On the road to Shur, she has a conversation that changes her life and her direction. The Lord tells her that He has heard of her misery, has seen her service, and understands her circumstances. Then God tells her submission must define the direction of her heart. Hagar turns around and goes back home. The situation hasn't changed. She has no reason to expect to be treated any differently. But a few words on the road lift the weight of invisibility off of Hagar's heart. Here's why. In Genesis 16:13, Hagar says, *"You are a God of seeing."*

God sees you. He notices what you do. He pays attention to how you move through your day. He sees you when you feel tired, unappreciated, used up, or unloved. He notices your quiet kindnesses, your effort to give your best, and your unseen sacrifices. He sees and He smiles. He notices and draws near. He pays attention and pours out His promises and purpose. He sees you. You can walk back into any circumstance you face today with the confidence and peace that comes from knowing that you are known and deeply loved.

My Jesus Resolution today is to really see someone around me. I am going to slow down and pay attention to the people who walk through my day. I want to listen, not just hear; see, not just glance; love, not just pass by. A hug, a note, a shoulder, or a smile may be all it takes to lift the weight of invisibility off of someone's heart today. God sees me. I want the way I interact with others today to help them see God.

You are not invisible today.
God sees you and loves you. How
can you help someone else see Him?

BATHTUB WATER

The most profound conversations always seem to happen in the car. We were driving to school, having a talk about the sun. It had reached the point with my preschool buddy that the answer had to be "because that is the way God made it." (Amazing how quickly a toddler can show you how little you really know!) His next question was, "Who is God?" A big question for a little guy.

How you answer this question is incredibly important. Here faith is boiled down to its essential elements. A.W. Tozer said, "What I believe about God is the most important thing about me."[2] He is right. What you believe about God will determine the depth of your surrender, the strength of your commitment, and the surety of your hope.

Wanting to give my little friend a wise answer, I replied, "God is the Lord of the heavens and the earth and the sky and the trees." He thought about this for a minute and said, "And bathtub water." God and I both just had to smile.

I wanted to give him a picture of God, but he gave me the wisest answer of all. He defined faith in simple terms, reminding me of the power of understanding who God is. God is the Lord of the heavens, earth, sky, and trees. Those are grand, majestic pictures. God is also the Lord of the places where I live, where I spend my time, where I am most vulnerable, and where I am the most at home. He is the Lord of bathtub water.

If God is Lord, He must be Lord of every part of me. He is Lord of the cosmos, world events, stunning vistas, and the stars beyond the stars. He is also Lord of my first cup of coffee, the way I look at myself in the mirror, what I watch on television, and the conversation I have with the clerk at the store. Big events. Small moments. He is Lord.

My Jesus Resolution today is to ask myself, "Who is God?" I want to think about His heart, see His character, imitate His nature, and look for His face in every part of my day. I want to surrender to the absolute truth that He is Lord – sovereign over each piece of my heart. I need to remember that there is no area of my life outside of His notice or desire or control. I want to walk through my day acknowledging that He is Lord of everything, especially bathtub water.

How do you need to let Jesus be more fully Lord of your bathtub water — the small, insignificant, unimportant, hidden parts of your day?

> *And beginning with Moses and all the Prophets, he interpreted to them in all the Scriptures the things concerning himself.* — Luke 24:27

Amazingly, we have a whole Bible full of testimony about Jesus. Some think that the record about Jesus begins in Matthew, but the truth is that the entirety of Scripture has one common theme. Every piece of the Bible points the way to Jesus and prepares our hearts to meet Him. For all its complexity and depth, the Bible speaks over and over to five basic truths.

1. The Bible tells us who God is.
2. The Bible tells us who we are.
3. The Bible tells us about sin and how it separates us from God.
4. The Bible tells us that Jesus is the answer to our deepest need.
5. The Bible tells us that we have an enemy.

At the root of each of these five basic truths, we find Jesus. He is God, and He reveals His heart to us. We are His beloved, the heart of His creation, made in His image. Sin tears us away from the heart of God, and Jesus becomes man in order to be the bridge that brings us back to Himself. Jesus stands victorious over the evil one who lives in rebellion and seeks to lure us away from God. Every word on every page of the Bible speaks to the unbounding love and amazing person of Jesus.

My Jesus Resolution today is to meet Jesus. Opening the pages of my Bible is a holy appointment with God. He meets me there. He uses its words to draw my eyes to His face and my heart to His heart. When I come to the Word of God, I need to come expecting transformation. These are the very words of God, and each one points to the Word who was in the beginning with God. When I open His book, He is speaking to me. I need to anticipate His presence. I need to expect His power. I need to understand that when I spend time in His Word – I will meet Jesus.

Memorize Psalm 119:105.
How will you let God's Word be a
light that helps you see Jesus today?

Excerpt from
Women Opening the Word
That You May Believe: The Gospel of John

TOUCHING BASE

She was just touching base. It has been a tough couple of weeks at college - tests taken, papers due, worrying about getting in the right classes for next year, fretting about dorms and roommates. A stress fracture knocked her out of a musical production she had been working on for months. I was more concerned about the stress fracturing her heart and her spirit.

It has been a couple of weeks of deep prayer. We have been asking God to touch every part of her day, every decision being made, every moment spent in study, and to make every minute she is stressed a time when she remembers she is blessed. Yesterday, the worry overflowed again. What if…? How come…? But why…? All she could see were the roadblocks and the obstacles. I wanted her to see God. We spent the next few minutes tracing God's handprint. We counted blessings, recalled answered prayers, and took inventory of the way He is moving and working on her behalf. We talked about His perfect timing, marveled in the shadow of open doors, and noticed His fingerprints on the mail.

Paying attention to the presence of God is about more than noticing where He is. It is a call to surrender our hearts to who He is. I wish I could tell you that all the worry dissipated. It didn't, but a couple of hours later I got a message. "It is all going to be okay." Peace is another mark of God at work. It happens when we open our eyes and hearts to His presence, and choose to rest in His hands.

My Jesus Resolution today is to touch base. I need to come back to center – the center of His presence, His will, and His mercy. I need to be reminded that He is in control. I need to remember deep love, unending grace, and timeless peace. I need to remember that the most important questions are not "Why?", "When?", or "Where?", but "Who?".

How will you center yourself in the heart of God today?

RECYCLING

Going green is big right now. People are concerned about the environment. There is a growing emphasis on reusing, reducing, and recycling. Taking care of our earth's resources is a necessary part of being good stewards of the blessings God has given us.

At our house, we recycle. We have a special bin that holds our aluminum cans, newspapers, and recyclable plastics. It has long been the job of our little ones to help take these items to the recycle bin. I have memory snapshots of little hands dropping one can at a time in the recycling bin, pride streaming across their faces as they learned the power of a job well done.

Despite the new emphasis on going green in our society, recycling is not a new idea. God has always been in the business of renewing, refreshing, recharging, redeeming, and redirecting. He loves taking the old and making it new. It is His deep desire to redeem the broken, infuse the used up with new purpose, and recycle our experiences into tools for His glory.

Nothing is wasted with God. He can take anything in our lives and use it to teach us about His heart. My job is to put what I have into His hands. Sometimes I look and all I see is trash – wasted, broken pieces of my attempts to do it on my own. In Romans 8:28, God makes an amazing promise to recycle our junk into good. *"And we know that for those who love God all things work together for good, for those who are called according to his purpose."* God's purpose is for me to look like Jesus. He will use everything I bring Him to make that transformation a reality in my life.

My Jesus Resolution today is to surrender to God's recycling plan. I am going to put my heart in His hands and ask Him to make me new. I am going to trust His faithfulness, surrender to His power, and believe His promises. He can take every part of me and renew it, reclaim it, repurpose it, and redeem it. Even the trash. Even the stuff that looks worthless, broken, and empty. He will use it all to create something brand new – a picture of Jesus in me.

What in your life do you need to ask God to recycle and renew?

FINDING PENNIES

We are penny pinchers. Not so much in the sense of being ultra-frugal (although we do cut out our fair share of coupons), but in the sense of picking up pennies we find on the ground. Are you one of those people? Do you stop in mid-step and pick up a penny, or do you let it pass?

Most people never see the penny in the first place. Eyes elsewhere, they completely miss the penny. Some people look at the ground and decide the penny isn't worth it. Others set a limit – they will pick up a dollar, but not a penny. Some people see a penny, stoop down, and put it in their pockets.

Pennies are like opportunities. They are the moments in time that God puts in our path. Perhaps they are chances to see Him, opportunities to show Jesus to someone, occasions to extend His grace and goodness, or openings to know more about His heart.

So many times I miss the penny. My focus is elsewhere, and I miss the moment when God is calling for my heart. Sometimes, I see the penny, but decide that it isn't worth breaking my stride or interrupting my schedule to pull it close. Other moments find me measuring the penny's worth. I want a big opportunity, a mountaintop experience, but a penny doesn't look like it holds much value. Once again, I miss God and all the riches He has in mind for me.

My Jesus Resolution today is to pick up a penny. I am going to make room for the moments when God calls for my attention and offers His presence. One hundred pennies make up a dollar. Taking the time to pick up pennies will make my eyes alert for His hands. It will cause my heart to be sensitive to the way He moves in my path. Bending down one hundred times may help my heart be softer and my soul more humble. Picking up pennies is how we build a storehouse of faith and how God shapes us to look like Jesus.

Carry a penny with you today as a reminder to pick up the pennies God puts in your path.

BAKING BREAD

I baked bread this morning. Just as the sun was beginning to color the sky, I peeked into the oven and saw the rising loaves taking shape. Turning on the oven, I started counting the minutes. The aroma of baking bread filled the house. Bread has its own unique, wonderful fragrance. The combination of flour, yeast, salt, and oil creates a mouth-watering, head-turning, nose-following smell. Yum!

Finally the timer signaled the end of the baking cycle. I pulled the warm loaves from the oven, setting them on a rack to cool. Opening the oven released an even stronger scent into the air. The aroma permeated the entire house. The smell of baking bread was enough to make tummies growl and smiles appear on morning faces.

Fast forward to later in the day. This was the moment that caught me by surprise. After a walk in the neighborhood, I pulled out my key to open our front door. Standing outside the house, I caught a familiar smell – baking bread. Our home was so full of the wonderful aroma that it leaked out of the house, filling the yard with its enticing smell.

The smell of baking bread always draws my mind to Jesus. He is the Bread of Life. He longs to nourish our souls in the same way delicious bread feeds our bodies. But it is the aroma that draws my eyes to His face. In 2 Corinthians 2:15 it says, *"For we are the aroma of Christ to God among those who are being saved and among those who are perishing."* Everywhere we go, we carry with us the fragrance of Christ. We have the opportunity to smell like Jesus for everyone we meet.

God taught me an important lesson today on the sidewalk. He wants me to be so full of the smell of the Living Bread that it spills out of my life, inviting those just walking by to experience it. I need to be so full of Jesus that it permeates every part of who I am.

My Jesus Resolution today is to be aware of how I smell. I want to leave the fragrance of Christ lingering in every room into which I walk. I am going to be especially careful not to let the smells of the world penetrate my heart. I want to open the doors of my life so that others can take a deep breath and smell the aroma of Christ in me.

How will you spread the aroma of Christ today?

TRASH TRUCKS

I am thankful for trash trucks today. Walking through my usual route in the neighborhood brought me behind the trash truck. Piles of garbage lined up by the sides of the road were disappearing into the truck as men hoisted trash cans filled with the garbage of life.

I don't spend a lot of time thinking about the trash truck. I take it for granted. It comes twice a week to haul off my junk. I discard the stuff I don't want, that I am finished with; or that is unusable, smelly, and broken. It goes into a bag and gets set by the curb for the trash truck to take away.

If all my garbage piled up in my life, it would be quite a mess. Rotting food, empty boxes, used containers, and broken dishes would not only be unsightly, it would stink. The aroma of garbage would begin to permeate where I live. The clutter of trash would overwhelm my life.

Sin is the garbage of our lives. It stinks. It piles up. It makes life miserable. It sits in mounds in our hearts as a monument to all that is broken and decaying in our lives.

Fortunately, we don't have to live like that. Jesus is willing to haul away all of our garbage. He takes our sin, hauling it off as far as the east is from the west. He gets rid of the stench of shame, the grime of guilt, and the burden of brokenness. He teaches us to grow in holiness and to breathe in the fragrance of faith. He opens the doors, cleans up the mess, and invests Himself in renovating our hearts.

My Jesus Resolution today is to be thankful for trash collection. Jesus is more than willing to get rid of the junk piling up in my life. Too often I want to hold on to what is stinky and broken. I imagine that somehow I am going to be able to fix it myself. Today I am going to put all of it in His hands. I will let Him recycle, reclaim, and renew everything for His glory.

What do you need to set by the curb and let Jesus haul away today?

TECHNICAL DIFFICULTIES

I'm stuck. I have been working on a new project for months. I have prayed, planned, and poured out my heart. We are so close to the finish line, I can almost taste it. Watching a dream become reality is an exciting, exhausting, exhilarating process. Each day the anticipation grows as ideas take shape and God's fingerprints on the project become more pronounced. But a computer virus has thrown my well-laid plans off track.

Without my permission, the virus attacked. One day, everything was going smoothly and we could see light at the end of the tunnel. The next day we couldn't find the tunnel. My interrupter was a computer virus, but it really could be anything that throws us off track, disturbs the balance of our days, throws us a curve, or derails our dreams. Sometimes it is something small – having to wait when we are in a hurry, losing our keys, or having a sick child on the day of an important meeting. Sometimes something huge – a relationship falling apart, the doctor coming in with a serious expression, or a pink slip waiting for us at work – changes the course of our lives. Interrupters happen. That much is sure. The question lies in how we will respond.

When the interrupter flares it lays my heart bare. Do I see myself as being in control of the moment, or do I find peace in the truth that God is in control of all my moments? I can get frustrated, angry, and grumpy, or I can search for God's movement, protection, and grace. God's timing is always perfect, His mercies are always new, His promises are always sure, and His presence is always with us. Even when viruses hit us unaware. God has seen tomorrow. He already knows what we will face and stands ready to walk with us through it all.

My Jesus Resolution today is take a deep breath and trust God's unchanging hand. Interrupters are going to be a part of my day. I want to learn to see God in each moment, recognize His presence, and rely on His power. A virus can't attack God's promises or undermine God's faithfulness. I want to ground my plans and dreams so thoroughly in the will of God that my confidence rests not on my abilities, but on His dependability.

How will you respond when technical difficulties come your way today?

DOOR OPENERS

My sons are learning to be door openers. We call them gentlemen-in-training. They have watched their grandfather do it for their grandmother, their dad do it for me, and now they are learning how to open doors for others. It is pretty neat to watch.

They are learning how to open car doors, front doors, garage doors, and store doors. There is a rhythm to learning how to open doors. You have to watch the other person. You have to be aware of how to move the door so that it is easiest for the person you are serving to go in and out. They are learning how to offer their hand or their arm if someone needs a little extra assistance. They are discovering how to pace themselves so that they can walk with someone and put them at ease.

I really can't think of anything else I would rather my children become than door openers. I want them to be able to open the doors of their hearts and love deeply. I want them to open the doors of their minds and drink in all the rich wisdom of God and the beauty of this world. I want them to open their eyes to the very real presence of God. I want their spirits to be open to the call of God on their lives, and their souls to be open to the transformation He wants to work deep within them.

I long for them to be door openers for others as they invite them into God's grace, to make it easier for someone to come to the cross and stand amazed by the empty tomb, to join in worship, and to bow in surrender.

I want the psalmist's desire to be the desire of their hearts. *"I would rather be a doorkeeper in the house of my God than dwell in the tents of wickedness"* (Psalm 84:10b).

My Jesus Resolution today is to be a door opener. I am going to learn from my sons. I am going to be deliberate about making it easier for someone to see Jesus. I want to open the door into His presence, invite someone to make themselves at home, and show someone the delight of His grace. Opening a door is such a simple thing. Yet, it is a gracious act that shows someone else they are important. Jesus was a door opener. My boys are learning. Now it is my turn.

For whom can you open a door today?

It is the only thing written in the back of my Bible. It simply says, "I don't know all the answers, but I know Someone who does."

We live in a world of questions. We live much of our lives in search of answers. Sometimes the questions are simple. At times, the questions touch the deepest part of who we are. Many times the questions echo our pain and confusion. There are moments when our questions call us to examine our hearts. So many questions.

Answers can be hard to come by. We sometimes struggle with our inability to answer the questions that define our lives. We think that having answers will give us a sense of peace or a shred of control over our lives. If we can just fit all the pieces together, make sense of it all, understand the whys, whens, and wheres that arise, we will be able to move forward.

The truth is we aren't always able to figure out all the answers. And that is okay. There are pieces I will never be able to fit together, mysteries I will never be able to solve, and circumstances I will never be able to control. I don't have all the answers, but I know Someone who does.

Deuteronomy 29:29 says, *"The secret things belong to the LORD our God, but the things that are revealed belong to us and to our children forever, that we may do all the words of this law."*

My Jesus Resolution today is to remember that my best answer is always Jesus. He sees all the whens. He is present in all the wheres. He knows the reasons for all the whys. I don't have to know all the answers. I just need to know Jesus. I can put all the pieces in His hands, trusting that He will fit them together in me in the way that best brings His image to bear in my life.

*How will you remember that
Jesus is the answer today?*

HIGHLIGHTERS

I like highlighters. I use them when I read. I hold a highlighter in my hand, using it to spotlight passages I want to remember, mark questions I want to ask, and note the words that help me see God more clearly.

Highlighters come in all shapes, colors, and sizes. Some work better with text books, others are made for thin pages, fine lines, or dark print. There are tiny ones, bright ones, big ones, neon ones, and classic ones. Go to the store and you will find a highlighter for all tastes, styles, and needs.

No matter what type of highlighter you choose, they all have one purpose. The purpose of a highlighter is not to cover up, but to add a layer that brings words into greater focus. In a word, they highlight. They spotlight. They draw attention to an idea.

People are like highlighters. We come in all different shapes, sizes, and colors. We have different talents, gifts, and quirks. We live in different places, have different responsibilities, and laugh at different things.

Yet, we have one purpose. Our job is to highlight God. Our lives are to serve as a spotlight on the majesty, holiness, power, faithfulness, and goodness of God. We are to make Him visible to the world. Our hearts are supposed to shine a spotlight on His grace so that others can see Him more clearly.

My Jesus Resolution today is to be a highlighter. My purpose is not to draw attention to myself. Like a highlighter, I need to be transparent so that what is within can shine through. I am going to be deliberate about drawing attention to the way God is at work around me. I am going to bring His name into focus. I am going to spotlight His handiwork. I am going to use my life to highlight the cross and help people see Jesus.

How will you be a highlighter today?

NANA BLANKETS

My mom made my kids two different kinds of quilts for their rooms when they were born.

The first kind is their crib quilts, but they are so much more to my kids. They call them their "nana blankets." Even though they have outgrown their cribs, these Nana Blankets are infinitely precious to them. They all sleep with their Nana Blankets. We have to take them with us when we travel. They have been washed a hundred times, thrown up on, and become wet with their tears. They have been used to chase away monsters, keep warm when chilled with fever, be a superhero, wrap baby dolls, and pick them up when the world has gotten them down. They can wrap up in those Nana Blankets and feel warm, safe, loved, and one hundred percent accepted because they know that when they are wrapped in their Nana Blankets, they are wrapped in their Nana's love.

The other kind of quilt she made for them is a wall-hanging quilt. They are beautiful. They hang by their beds and decorate their rooms. People come in and "ooh and aah" over them. But they get dusty. They cannot play with them or touch them. We don't travel with them; they stay at home.

In a fire, which one do you think my children would save? I don't even have to ask. They would save the soft, warm, not so pristine Nana Blankets.

I have learned a lesson about Jesus from watching my kids with their quilts. Is Jesus my wall hanging or my Nana Blanket? Does He hang on a wall, decorate my life, never get touched, get rather dusty, and sometimes look out of place? Or is He a little worn around the edges from being held so tight, loved on, laughed with, and soaked with tears?

My Jesus Resolution today is to make Jesus my Nana Blanket. I want to hang on to Him, determine to take Him with me wherever I go, and never let Him out of my sight. I want Him to be a part of every activity in my day. He is able to dry away my tears. Most of all, when I wrap Him around me, I will feel safe and loved and completely accepted and cherished.

Is Jesus a wall hanging in your life or your Nana Blanket?

Excerpt from
Women Opening the Word
The Fragrance of Faith:
Discovering the Aroma of Christ in the Beatitudes

God showed me something important about my heart this morning. My dog and I were out for our morning walk. We get up early, starting our rounds as the sun comes peeking over the horizon. My dog walks faithfully by my left side. She sticks close, and we enjoy the time together before the busyness of the day sets in.

Shelby (my dog) doesn't like sprinklers. She was a rescue dog so we don't know what happened in her past that made sprinklers the enemy, but she is terrified of them. She watches for them. She can hear the sound of a sprinkler turning on a half a block away. And she goes out of her way to avoid them.

Walking early in the morning inevitably means we encounter sprinklers. This morning, the gushing of a sprinkler sent Shelby scrambling. She moved from my left side to my right side. Not a big move from her perspective, but for me it was scary. A car was coming up fast on my right side.

Shelby is okay, but God used the moment to teach me an important lesson. How many times do I scramble to avoid something that makes me uneasy, only to move into a far more dangerous situation? God wants me to stay by His side. Sometimes He has me walk into circumstances that I would rather avoid because walking another way would not be what is best for me. I grumble and complain about the sprinkler, while God has His eye on the speeding car.

My Jesus Resolution today is to trust God in the sprinkler moments of life. In walking by His side, I will always be safe. He will lead me the right way. He will guide my steps and guard my paths. He is watching out for my best, moving me in the way that is going to bring me closer to His heart. I might have to walk through a sprinkler today, but I am going to trust God's perspective rather than listening to my own wisdom. I would rather get a little wet with God, than try to walk it on my own.

How will you trust God in your sprinkler moments today?

COMING SOON

There is a new restaurant opening in my neighborhood. The signs are up, the construction and prep crews are working, and excitement is building. We are looking forward to its arrival. Every time we drive past the location, we point it out. We talk about what it is going to be like, what will be on the menu, and how it will compare to our current favorites.

A "Coming Soon" sign hangs from the store front. It is a promise and an invitation. It is a promise that the preparations underway will soon allow the doors to open and business to begin. It is an invitation to prepare, to get ready, to set our eyes on the moment the doors open. It is a promise to take up residence in our lives and become a part of our landscape. It is an invitation to come in, sit down, and enjoy the food.

In Revelation 22:7, Jesus says, *"And behold, I am coming soon."* All of the excitement and anticipation wrapped up in a new restaurant opening should help me refocus on the greatest promise and invitation of all.

Jesus is coming soon. In His words, we hear a promise. He has gone to prepare a place for us. Construction is in progress, preparations are underway, and all things are being made ready. Soon the doors of heaven will be thrown open and the real joy of living in God's presence will begin. In the meantime, He takes up residence in our lives, changing the landscapes of our hearts and getting us ready for the moment when He will arrive.

There is also an invitation in His "coming soon" promise. It is an invitation to prepare and get ready. It is an invitation to anticipate and to be excited about His "coming soon" day. It is an invitation to investigate, be curious, and peek in the windows. It is an invitation to come in, sit down, and enjoy the banquet He is preparing just for you.

My Jesus Resolution today is to anticipate His "coming soon" with more intensity. His promise should color how I look at my schedule, my checkbook, and my priorities. Anticipation should wake me up in the morning. Excitement should flow into my conversation. Preparation should define my days. Today I get an opportunity to invite others into His "coming soon" promise. Today "coming soon" is going to inspire me to look more like Jesus.

How will you anticipate His "coming soon" today?

IDENTITY THEFT

Someone I love has been touched by identity theft. A routine check revealed that someone has invaded my daughter's privacy and is using her personal information. In a single moment, her name was being used, her integrity questioned, and her sense of security shaken. We were blessed. There hasn't been a lot of damage done. No money is missing. We are following law enforcement procedures, wading through the paperwork to set things right.

Nothing is more central to how we walk through our days than our identity. It defines us, guides us, sets our priorities, and shapes our days. Our identity is at the core of who we are and is the lens through which we see and interact with the world. Being a Christian means, at its heart, that our identity is defined by Jesus. He names us, claims us as His own, purchases our freedom, and calls us His children. Our identity is rooted in the cross, empowered by His blood, and defined by His love. It shapes our perspective and gives us new eyes.

Satan is the ultimate identity thief. He wants us to question who we are, doubt where we belong, and fear the One who calls us His own. His greatest desire is for us to take on one of the many identities offered by the world – to define ourselves by power, money, education, or beauty. Anything but God. He pulls at our hearts and tries to strip away the confidence we have in wearing the name of Jesus.

Our daughter is learning the necessity of protecting her identity. We need to learn to do the same.

My Jesus Resolution today is to be vigilant about protecting, guarding, and living within the identity I have in Jesus. I am not going to let thieves tear me away from the purpose God is working out in my life. I am going to safeguard my soul from those trying to sneak in to steal my joy, confidence, and peace. To protect my identity, I am going to keep myself rooted in the cross, define my heart by His character, and keep my eyes open for His presence. I am a Christian – God's beloved. Nobody can steal that from me.

How can you protect yourself from spiritual identity theft today?

I just finished a new quilt. I put the final stitches in, pulled the basting threads, and spread it out on the floor to admire it. It is so neat to see how pieces of fabric, batting, and thread come together to create something beautiful. On their own, each piece of the quilt looks insignificant. Most are small. They are cut at funny angles. Crooked edges are mixed in with straight ones. Some of the pieces are brightly colored and eye catching. Many are in ordinary, nothing-special hues. But put them together, use a needle and thread, invest some time, and the results are extraordinary.

One of the reasons I love quilts is because they are a reminder for me of the way God is working in my life. Our days, our choices, our relationships, and our surrender are the pieces of fabric. Occasionally, there is a spectacular one, but most are ordinary by themselves. We look at our days, like them, but don't always see their beauty. Only when they come together in the pattern God is working into our lives can we stand back and catch our breath in wonder.

Quilting requires dealing with knots, untangling thread, stretching the fabric in a frame, and using scissors. The struggles, stresses, knots, and tangles of our days are a part of our quilt. Each one is part of the process of putting together something beautiful. Each marks a moment when God is working His grace into the fabric of our lives.

Quilts tell a story. Each one is unique. Every quilt bears the mark of the person who held it in their hands. Time, energy, creativity, and love are woven into its design. No one makes a quilt by accident. God is using every piece of your life to make something that will reflect His beauty. He is using the pattern of His own heart to take the ordinary, average pieces of our days and turn them into something that will help the world see Jesus.

My Jesus Resolution today is to open my eyes to the way God is putting the pieces of my heart together for His glory. He is going to use each piece, each experience, each surrender, each prayer, each moment spent in service, each sacrifice, and each person who touches my day to imprint His pattern deep into my quilt. There will be knots to untangle, stretching to do, and needles to thread, but each moment rests in the hands of the Master Quilter.

What will you sew into this day for Him?

LOST

I got lost yesterday. I went straight when I should have turned right and ended up west of somewhere I didn't want to be. I never did make it to where I was supposed to go. I am still shaking my head at how I got so turned around.

Life is like that – we turn left instead of right, we end up someplace we didn't plan on going, something happens that disrupts our schedules and good intentions. In those moments, we have a choice. Close our eyes in frustration or open them wide and search for God. So often, we get caught up in beating ourselves up for making the wrong turn. When things don't go as planned, we turn our eyes to ourselves and examine the mess that now defines our day. Stuff happens. Life throws us curve balls. We end up missing the turn and miss seeing God in the unexpected places or circumstances we find ourselves in.

But He is there and His presence has the power to redeem our day. Yesterday was a great day – not the day I planned – but a day filled with treasures from God. No matter what happens today – look for God, trace His fingerprints on your minutes, be especially aware of His nearness. The other stuff is going to happen. Only you can decide whether you are going to let it pull you down or open your eyes to seeing Him.

My Jesus Resolution today is to see my wrong turns with the right eyes. I want to walk with Jesus and learn more about experiencing the fullness of His presence. Learning to see Him in difficult circumstances, lost moments, and wrong turns helps me trace His hand and show others His fingerprints. I don't often plan for the difficult things that come my way, but seeing Him in the wrong turns helps me see every moment as an opportunity to look like Jesus.

How will you let God use your "lost" moments to pull you closer to His heart?

DRIVING

I got to ride in the car with a toddler this week. I had forgotten how special those times in the car could be. He demanded an ongoing conversation. He wanted to comment on everything, ask about whatever came to his mind, and look in wonder at dump trucks, school buses, and helicopters. Usually, driving my car is about getting from point A to point B. I turn on some music, put the car into drive, and focus on reaching my destination. My little friend's joy came from enjoying the journey. We sang the traffic light song at every light. We squealed with delight looking for cherry pickers. We counted dump trucks traveling down the road and wondered where they might be headed. The drive became an adventure because he challenged me to pay attention.

How often do we live in autopilot? Going through our routines, walking through our days focused on getting to the next place and crossing the next thing off the list? How much beauty, wonder, and just plain fun do we miss because we don't really stop to pay attention? Jesus challenges us to do just that – slow down and look. See His fingerprints on the world around us and catch our breath in wonder. Enjoy the moment because this is where God is present.

My Jesus Resolution today is to slow down and enjoy the ride. I am going to pay attention, really pay attention, to the ways God is making Himself known all around me. I want to look for beauty, watch for wonder, and find joy in the journey. His fingerprints can be found in every moment. Each one reveals His deep love and His plan to bring me home. God has an adventure planned for me today. I am looking forward to the drive.

How will you turn off the autopilot today and take joy in your journey?

AWFUL

It has been an awful day. You know the kind. The nothing-goes-right, everything-falls-apart, what-else-could-go-wrong-but-it-does-anyway kind of day. We walk through days like that and cringe. It seems like the cards are stacked against us, someone has our number, and we are wearing a "Kick Me" sign on our backs. Awful days. Days in which we can't wait to close our eyes, and let the calendar page turn.

What if we could turn awful days into awe-full days? Awful days are going to happen. That doesn't mean that they have to be awe-empty days. Perhaps, more than any other kind of day, we need to learn how to infuse awful days with awe. Maybe a little awe is the antidote to awful.

Awe flows from being aware. During awful days, our eyes turn inward. We fill our vision with our circumstances, our feelings, our inadequacies, and our sense of being out-of-control. Filling our days with awe begins by looking up, searching the landscape for His presence, and being aware that His promises are in full force.

When we catch a glimpse of His hand, it becomes easier to move into the second facet of awe – worship. Worship acknowledges that God is in control, that we can trust His goodness and surrender to His movement. Praise draws our hearts out of our circumstances and focuses our souls on the ever-present, ever-loving, ever-faithful nature of our Lord.

Worship draws us to make the third step into awe – engage. When we engage in His call on our lives, we infuse even the most awful days with a higher purpose. The focus of our days becomes more than survival. Each one takes on a divine sense of mission, allowing Him to shape the day for His glory.

My Jesus Resolution today is the have an awe-full day. I want to remain aware of how He is moving in my day. I want my eyes to be open and my heart to be driven by praise. I want to lift my heart to His throne and take on the fullness of His purpose. No matter how awful my day is, it is a day in which I can look like Jesus. Focusing on Jesus will turn awful into awe-full.

How will you commit to having an awe-full day today?

We are people bound by time. We can't escape it. It permeates our perspective, priorities, and perceptions. Sometimes, time "flies." Other occasions seem to exaggerate the ticking of the clock. The years with our children go by very quickly even as days filled with homework, little sleep, practices, and toys find us watching for bedtime to arrive.

God exists outside of time. He created it, and uses it for His purposes. Because God is not bound by time, His perspective is different than ours. He works in time for our good. From my viewpoint, it often seems that God is moving too slowly. I want an answer, some intervention, a little miracle, a great measure of peace, a dose of grace, or a big bunch of patience right now!

This weekend I heard someone say – "God is right on time, every time, all the time." It was a truth of which I needed to be reminded. I get frustrated by time, defined by time, measured by time, and even ruled by time. Yet, time is held in the hands of God. He will use time as a blessing in our lives to draw us closer to Himself. God handles time according to the nature of His heart – with justice, goodness, truth, and love. Whatever our perspective may be, God is right on time, every time, all the time.

My Jesus Resolution today is to trust God's timing. Jesus rested in God's timing completely. He moved according to God's will and walked in the timing of God's purpose. God works in time for my good. No matter what today brings, God is never impatient, never restricted by the clock, and never late. He is always right on time.

How can you more fully trust God's timing today?

UNFADING BEAUTY

> *But let your adorning be the hidden person of the heart with the imperishable beauty of a gentle and quiet spirit, which in God's sight is very precious.* —1 Peter 3:4

A gentle spirit is one that has learned to lean wholly on God. A woman with a gentle spirit is humble and has surrendered to the will and purpose of God in her life. She is the woman who enters a room, filling it with light. She wears the aroma of Christ and its sweet scent lingers behind her. She walks with you through difficult times, and you feel encouraged and renewed just because she is there. A gentle spirit chooses to direct your attention to the presence and work of God in your life, and encourages you to more closely walk with Him.

God combines the qualities of gentle humility and trust with quietness. This unfading beauty does not need to call attention to itself or feel the need to flaunt every move. Quietness dispels the whining, complaining, worry, and moodiness in which we often indulge. It is a spirit that knows how to be still before God. It moves to rest itself in the presence of God. It develops eyes to see His hand at work in every moment. It learns to listen to His voice and surrender to His will. It buffs away the calluses of a hard heart and complaining spirit. A woman with a gentle and quiet spirit is very aware of God's hand on her life, and moves under His power and in rhythm with His heartbeat.

The beauty of a gentle and quiet spirit is developed in small, daily moves of submission. It is the makeover of a lifetime.

My Jesus Resolution today is to commit myself to unfading beauty. I am going to let every part of my beauty routine be a reminder to let God unfold His beauty within me. When I shower, I am going to recommit myself to holiness and purity. I want to let my toothbrush and toothpaste remind me to be gentle, encouraging, and uplifting with every word I say. My hairbrush can help me remember how He cares for every hair on my head. I am going to let the scent of my perfume remind me to carry the aroma of Christ with me into every situation. As I get dressed, I am going to clothe myself with Christ.

How will you commit yourself to unfading beauty today?

Excerpt from
Women Opening the Word
Echoing His Heartbeat: The Life of David

It was a quiet morning—a time spent pouring my heart out to God. Needs of all shapes and sizes were pressing on my heart. As my worries and concerns came tumbling out, I tried to slow down and quiet my heart. I didn't want to present God with a laundry list of requests. I wanted to meet God, let Him speak to my heart, and open my eyes to His presence and movement.

His answer came not in specific fixes for my concerns, but in pointing my eyes to His heart. Genesis 22:14 tells of a moment of desperate need, unspeakable heartache, and surrender wrapped in sacrifice. In that moment, God points Abraham to Himself and reveals that He is Jehovah-Jireh – The Lord Will Provide. His very name is the answer.

Leafing through the needs pressing on my heart, I realized they were all requests for provision of one kind or another. For some, I was begging for peace, grace, healing, or a special measure of His nearness. For others, I was seeking an open door, open eyes, or an open heart. There were physical needs to be met, inspiration needed, and transformation required. In every instance, God answered that He is Jehovah-Jireh – The Lord Will Provide.

Philippians 4:19 tells us exactly how God is prepared to provide for us. *"And my God will supply every need of yours according to his riches in glory in Christ Jesus."* It is the little word *every* that shows the big power of our God. He is willing and able to provide for every need, meet every heartache, answer every concern, and fill every moment with Himself.

My Jesus Resolution today is to rest in the presence and power of my Provider. I am going to let Philippians 4:19 resonate throughout my day. The Lord stands in my day and promises to meet all my needs. The big ones, the little ones, the silly ones, and the serious ones. He will meet my needs not because I have it all together, can answer all the questions, or juggle all the balls, but according to His unlimited, inexhaustible and glorious riches. What do you need today? The Lord Will Provide.

Read Philippians 4:19.
Write it on your heart. Let it speak
to you today as you depend on Him
to provide all you need.

LITTLE THINGS

My grandmother gave me a little poem that still whispers in the back of my mind.

The little things are most worthwhile –
A quiet word, a secret smile,
A cheerful laugh, a helping hand,
A look that says "I understand"
A listening ear that's quick to share
Another's thoughts, another's cares.
Although sometimes these things
May seem quite small,
The little things mean most of all.
- Author unknown

My grandmother taught me the value of simple kindnesses. She showed me that small, gentle touches on someone's day really do make a difference. Little things have a lot of power to change our perspective, relieve our loneliness, and lift our spirits.

God works in the same way. Our days are filled with "little things" that speak to His presence and proclaim His love. It is often in the quiet moments that God speaks to our hearts. He gently touches our days in simple, small ways that seek to remind us that He is here and that He cares.

My Jesus Resolution today is watch for little things. I am going to make a special effort to watch for the little ways God is touching my day. I am going to add up all the times I see Him move in simple, quiet places. I am going to celebrate the little things today and let that celebration overflow into praise for my very big God.

What little things will catch your eye today reminding you that God loves you and that He is close to your heart?

COMING HOME

Our daughter is home for a school break. It is always a joy to see her smile. She brings beauty and laughter with her every time she enters a room. Her presence around the dinner table makes us feel complete.

It is in her attitude about coming home that I most clearly see Jesus. She is thriving in college – making friends, stretching her heart, and soaking in the education she has dedicated herself to achieving. But she is very aware that school is not home. It is a temporary place. There is much to be embraced, absorbed, and enjoyed about college. She loves it, but lives with the reality that it is not a permanent home for her heart. It is a training place, a learning place, a growing place, and a blessing place. She commits herself to living in the moment, but always has her eye on when it will be time to come home.

I want to be like her. I want to see my surroundings as the temporary dwelling that it really is. I want to long for home the way she does. Living with a "coming home" perspective changes my priorities. I don't need to invest myself so heavily in the temporary things of this world. I can look at my circumstances, struggles, and to-do lists with eyes that long for home. This life is a training place, a learning place, and a growing place. Here I learn to look like Jesus. Here I am shaped to walk with Him, grow in Him, and imitate Him. Here I learn to long for home.

My Jesus Resolution today is to point my heart toward home. I am going to spend time today thinking, reading, and praying about home. I am going to connect with my Father who is getting things ready for me. I am going to look at the events of my day with eyes focused on home. I am going to let my desire to see Jesus color every part of who I am. I can't wait until it is time come to home.

*How will you point your heart
toward home today?*

ACORNS

Looking out my kitchen window, I can see an oak tree. It is a small oak tree. My son started with an acorn and a determination to grow a tree of his very own. He planted the acorn, waiting and watching with the faith of a child for his tree to grow.

My son has big plans for this tree. It is going to be big enough for a fort, tree house, and "no girls allowed" clubhouse. I haven't quite had the heart to tell him that it will be his grandchildren building those things in the tree. Right now the tree is only about three feet tall.

But he has the right idea. He has learned that God can take something small and make it into something grand, something substantial, and something worth building dreams on.

I look at the tree and see a picture of my heart. In our hurry-up society, we want instant oak trees. But that isn't the way oak trees grow. They take time to mature, to send roots deep into the soil, and to fulfill all the potential wrapped up in an acorn.

Jeremiah 17:7-8 contains an amazing promise for those of us who feel more like acorns than mature oaks. *"Blessed is the man who trusts in the LORD, whose trust is the LORD. He is like a tree planted by water, that sends out its roots by the stream, and does not fear when heat comes, for its leaves remain green, and is not anxious in the year of drought, for it does not cease to bear fruit."*

My Jesus Resolution today is to stop trying to rush God's work in my life. He is creating a reflection of Christ in me that is meant to stand sure and strong for a lifetime. It takes time for His transformation to take deep root in my heart. Just as He holds the maturing of an oak tree in His hands, so He also holds me. All of His plans, creativity, power, and purpose will come to fruition in my life in His time and in His way. My job is to believe and dream about the possibilities that exist inside every acorn.

Have you ever tried to rush God's work in your life? How did you learn to trust in His timing and plan?

PICTURE FRAMES

We were looking for the perfect frame. We had taken the best picture of hugs, smiles, and giggles, and wanted to preserve the memory. Now we were looking for a frame so that we could share the picture with friends. It had to be just right. We searched the store for a frame that fit the picture and captured the essence of the playful moment.

We walked around the store holding our picture. Some of the frames were big and flashy. Other frames were covered in poetry and words of wisdom. Some featured exotic woods, bright colors, and embellishments of feathers and rhinestones. None seemed to fit just right.

Frame shopping taught me a lesson about living for Jesus. When looking for a frame, we wanted one that complimented our picture and drew eyes to the faces captured on film. We wanted the focus to be the smiles, the laughter, and the love. I didn't want people looking at the frame and missing the picture. I don't want people looking at me and missing Jesus.

I am a frame. Jesus is the picture. My purpose is to help people see the picture. It is fine for the frame to be pretty, or poetic, or have a dash of bling, unless those things draw the viewer's eyes away from the picture. When the frame starts competing with the picture, it is time to reevaluate. When the frame begins to think that it is supposed to be the focal point, it is time to remind of ourselves of God's purpose for our hearts.

My Jesus Resolution today is be a great frame. I want people to look at Jesus when they see my life. I want to compliment His movement, echo His words, and imitate His heart. I am going to remember that my purpose is to frame Jesus and display Him to the world.

How can you best frame Jesus in your life today?

WATER

It was a cryptic message. "We have had a little excitement here." It wasn't the words I wanted to hear coming home after a long day at work. "What kind of excitement?" I asked, half hoping to hear that the million dollars we had been promised for years by the envelope in the mail had finally shown up at our door. That wasn't it. What I heard instead was, "We don't have any water."

A small outside pipe had corroded and was gushing water into the yard. A utility man driving by saw the problem and turned the water off at the main. A very helpful neighbor pitched in, and the problem was solved pretty quickly. Now we had to wait for the water to be turned back on.

We waited. And waited. And waited.

During the time we waited, God opened our eyes. We take clean water for granted. We don't pay much attention to the blessing of running water. We turn on the faucet, do our thing, and move on. We miss opportunities to see Jesus in something as ordinary as the water coming through our faucets.

Yet, each drop of water should point us to His face. He is the Living Water. He refreshes our spirits with His love. His grace fills in the cracks left by despair and discouragement. He fills us to overflowing with His goodness. He calls us to dive into the deep waters of His mercy and faithfulness. He runs through my life like water runs through my house— always there, always available, always ready, always close.

My Jesus Resolution today is to appreciate water. I am going to turn on the sink, grateful that Jesus is always present in my life. I am going to take a shower, rejoicing in the way He cleanses me and makes me new. I am going to enjoy a cold glass of water, pausing to praise His name for filling my soul with Himself. Maybe there will be a little excitement here today in how many times I glimpse Him when I turn on the water.

Read John 7:37-38.
How can water help you be
thankful for Christ's presence in
your life today?

I SHALL NOT BE MOVED

I have a song playing in my head today. The words written by Edward H. Boatner proclaim, "Glory hallelujah, I shall not be moved; Anchored in Jehovah, I shall not be moved; Just like a tree that's planted by the waters, I shall not be moved."[3]

It is an interesting song. Usually, we talk about walking with God, being open to His work in our lives, and being aware of His movement. This song plants our feet at the foot of the cross, declaring that we will not move from its shadow.

Our world is trying to lure us away from the cross. Subtly at times, by millimeters or inches, we hear enticements to depend on our own righteousness, create our own joy, and find our own answers. Sometimes the invitation is a siren call, drowning out the still, small voice that invites us into His presence.

Every day there is a time and place to sing "I Shall Not Be Moved." Maybe it is when we are faced with temptation, weary and tired from the burdens of the day, or faced with a choice between surrender and self-satisfaction. Each time we take a stand, wrap our arms around the cross, and declare that we will not be moved, our roots sink a little deeper into the rich soil of His love.

My Jesus Resolution today is to sing "I Shall Not Be Moved" out loud. While I want to move closer to Christlikeness, move further into His heart, and move more confidently in His will, I don't ever want to move outside of His presence. I don't want to take one step out of the shadow of His love and purpose for me. "I Shall Not Be Moved" is an anthem that declares that no matter the intensity of the storm, the darkness of the night, or the strength of the hardship, I am going to plant my heart at the foot of the cross. Want to sing with me?

Where do you most need to sing "I Shall Not Be Moved" today?

HAMMERS

"Please bring a hammer to Bible class on Sunday." That's all that the postcard said. My daughter was very excited because it was mail addressed specifically to her. She was two and getting a card from her Sunday school teacher was enough to generate smiles, giggles, and grins.

I was a little skeptical. Had the teacher thought through the reality of a room full of two-year-olds swinging hammers? What if they hit each other rather than the wood? What if they dropped it on their toes? What if…?

My husband thought it was a great idea. He and my daughter set out on an adventure to the hardware store. He bought a hammer just for her. It was small enough to fit her hand and light enough for her to carry. I am not sure who was more proud.

Sunday morning rolled around and there was my sweet daughter as excited as she could be. She was dressed in her pink dress, matching bow, little sandals, carrying her Bible and her hammer. It was time for church. She was not going to be late.

I dropped her off with her teacher, eyeing the room for the first aid kit. Other parents were looking in warily. Kids brought in hammers of all shapes and sizes.

I will admit to a little parental monitoring. I hung around and peeked in the window, and what I saw took my breath away. With her Bible open, the teacher told them the story of Jesus. With patience and love, she helped each one hold the hammer and hit a nail. With a hammer and a big heart, she helped them take the first steps into looking like Jesus.

My Jesus Resolution today is to hold a hammer. Jesus was a carpenter. He built things. He still does. He is willing to build holiness into my life. He longs to erect patience, love, and humility in my heart. He is able to tear down the walls that hide me from His grace. Holding a hammer in my hand is a tangible reminder to imitate Him in everything I do. I am thankful for the people He has put in my life to help me do that. I want to be just as excited as my daughter was to do exactly what Jesus would do. If I do, I have hit the nail on the head.

Who is someone that has helped you learn how to better look like Jesus? Thank them today.

THE HUG

There was a big crowd in the hallway. People were gathered around, talking, sharing, laughing, and comparing weather reports. In the middle of the crowd was one child. Dwarfed by all the grown-ups around him, my little friend was watching intently for something. His eyes searched the faces of the people around him, even as he stood still near his dad.

I walked toward the clamor of voices, grinning at the group. They filled the hallway, spilling over into the entryway. I was getting ready to walk around the other direction when I saw him. I watched him for a moment as he interacted with the adults intent on coaxing a giggle from him. He spotted me, and a huge smile filled his face. He pulled away from his dad's side and headed straight into my arms. He buried himself in my neck, holding on extra tight.

We whispered to each other for a couple of minutes. We talked about his plans for the afternoon, when he could next come over to play, and what he might have for lunch. It was a moment to touch base. A moment to reconnect and be reassured of love. It was a moment of blessing as he once again taught me how to approach Jesus.

His lesson was simple - keep your eyes open for Jesus even as you stand in the world. I love the fact that he knew who he was looking for. The moment he saw me, he headed to my side. A shared moment of love made us both more ready to face the rest of the day.

My Jesus Resolution today is to imitate my little friend. I am going to keep my eyes open for Jesus. I don't want to get so caught up in what is going on around me that I miss Him. I want our hearts to connect. I need to hear His voice. I long to throw myself into His arms, knowing that in that embrace I am safe, loved, and blessed.

How will you keep your eyes open for Jesus today?

> *Now Jesus was praying in a certain place, and when he finished, one of his disciples said to him, "Lord, teach us to pray...."*
> — Luke 11:1

Do you remember your child's first word? Children learn language by listening to their parents. They watch us and observe the way we speak. They mimic sounds and see the delight on our faces as we interact. As they grow and develop, they imitate the sounds that they hear and wait for a response. Finally the day comes when they say their first recognizable word. We hope for "mama" or "dada." My daughter's first word was "dog" but that didn't lessen the excitement. Learning to communicate with each other opens up a whole new world and is the foundation upon which the depths of our relationships rest.

Learning to pray is much like a child learning to speak. It is something that we can and must learn how to do. No one is born speaking. No one is born praying. We learn to communicate with God in much the same way that children learn to communicate with those around them. We learn the language of prayer by listening to our Father. We watch and observe the way that He speaks, and learn to communicate by following His example.

Many people feel intimidated by prayer. We worry that our language is not grand enough, our thoughts are not lofty enough, our words are not spiritual enough, and our focus is not pious enough. Set your worry down. God delights in your words to Him in the same way that you delight in listening to a little one speak those first new words. As much as you enjoy talking and visiting with your best friend, God enjoys spending time with you. You don't worry about being profound as you sit over coffee and share your life. You speak from the heart.

Sometimes there are tears; often there is laughter. You talk about daily delights as well as deep difficulties. In the company of your friend, silence sometimes communicates more than words. If you can talk to your best friend, then you can pray.

My Jesus Resolution today is to ask God to teach me to pray. I want the ease and transparency of close friendship to define the way I pray. I long for prayer to become a place of deep connection. I want to pour myself out and open my heart to the way He wants to fill me with Himself. Jesus doesn't leave me to figure it out on my own, but will teach me to pray so that I can look more like Him.

What would you most like to learn about prayer? Ask Him to teach you.

Excerpt from
Women Opening the Word
Our Father in Heaven... Teach Us to Pray

MRS. SMITH

I haven't thought about her in a long time. This morning I was watching a young mother, arms filled with all the paraphernalia that comes with babyhood, maneuver through the chairs after Bible class, and it all came flashing back.

It was a Sunday morning. I had a baby in one arm, a Bible in my other hand, and a diaper bag and purse swinging from each shoulder. I was making my way across the auditorium. To be honest, I think I must have had a look of desperation on my face. Exhaustion marked my steps as a long night of fussiness caught up with both of us. It was one of those mornings when I wondered why I even bothered.

Mrs. Smith caught me about halfway across the auditorium. She was an older lady. Sweet and caring, she always paused to say hello and coo over the baby. We greeted each other, and I began to continue my move to a back pew where I could get out easily when the baby got fussy. As I began to walk away, she touched my arm ever so lightly. I turned back, and she whispered five words. "You're doing a great job." She patted my arm and went on her way.

All of the sudden my morning looked different. Her reassurance went straight to my heart and chased away my doubts and insecurities. Her encouragement made a difference for this young mother. And she taught me a valuable lesson.

She said just five words. That's it. But she spoke them at a moment of deep need. Years later, I still remember the impact they had on me. Sometimes we don't see encouragement as a very noble gift. It is just a card, a phone call, a hug, or a word. It doesn't seem like much in the moment, but to the person on the receiving end of that encouragement, it can mean the world.

My Jesus Resolution today is to be an encourager. I am going to make the phone call, send the card, and give the hug. It is a seed of grace that I can plant in someone's day. I will never know how God is going to use those words to lift someone's heart towards Him. I never thanked Mrs. Smith. She probably never knew how she pointed me to God that day. So thank you, Mrs. Smith. You made a difference with just five words.

How will you be deliberate today about offering someone encouragement?

THE LINE

I walked into the kitchen and had to hide a smile. There was my son working diligently on the floor. He had been in there for quite a while. He had a plan, and he was working at it with all his might. At three-years-old, he was diligently making a line of baby food jars. He had taken all of his little brother's baby food jars out of the cabinet and was putting them in order across the kitchen floor.

I wish you could have seen it. It was a long line, an exact line. Every jar had a place. Every jar was in a sequence. I am not sure of his goal, but he was working at lining up those jars with everything he had.

Then came the tears. "It's time to put the jars back in the pantry." He looked at me in disbelief. Didn't I see the masterpiece laid out across the kitchen? Couldn't I see how hard he had worked? Surely, I noticed the genius in the placement of the line.

His line showed me a truth about my heart. I spend so much time making plans, arranging details, and organizing my line. I lay it all out, have a vision in my head, and expect others to see the genius in my way of thinking. Especially God. Many times, God has a different plan for me. I pout and fuss because I have worked so hard at my line. I question His wisdom, while looking at my line with pride.

God's plans for me are so much better than the plans I can come up with for myself. He sees the opportunities I would miss. He knows the dangers I might face. Most importantly, His plan is the most direct path for creating within me the image of Jesus. If I take another road, follow my own path, or create my own line, I will have filled my time but missed the way God wants to work within me.

My Jesus Resolution today is to give God my line. I am going to organize my life around His purpose. I want to wait and listen before lining up my jars. I long to have eyes that see His plan taking shape in my life. My line leads nowhere. God's line always leads straight to His heart.

Read Proverbs 16:9.
How will you let the Lord
establish your steps today?

They are playing Scrabble in the other room. Gathered around a checkered board, they put words together, add up points, call for the dictionary, and laugh. It is a neat picture, one that captures more than the essence of a game. It is the essence of life.

Scrabble is a game that demands you take the letters you are given; use the language, vocabulary, and learning that you have poured into your life; and put words together. We are all given letters in life. Pieces that we are supposed to take and make into something meaningful. Not only do we have to come up with words, they have to fit on the board and mesh with everyone else's words. But here is the opportunity – we can choose the words that we create.

Every day, we get a new set of letters. We can complain about the letters we are given and refuse to play. We can roll our eyes, throw down a three-letter word, and pass our turn. We can plan and plot, and then get frustrated when somebody takes our play. Or we can get creative, take inspiration from the words that others have laid down before us, and make the best out of what is in our hand.

The truth is that words have power. Words can build up or tear down. They can give life or cut away at someone's heart. We can choose the words we put on the board, committing to creating words with our lives that will point others to Jesus.

My Jesus Resolution today is to build words that will last. I am going to fill my mind with God's words so that they will be there for me to draw on when I look at my letters. I am going to see the opportunities to seek His face that are built into my hand. I am going to build on what the people around me have already discovered about how to walk with God, letting their letters become part of my life's words. I can't wait to see the letters I get today. I know that God is in control of my day. Whatever happens, He will pour out enough grace so that I can find the letters J-E-S-U-S.

*The letters of life are the opportunities
that we are given each day.
What will you spell with yours?*

THE POWER IS ON

The storm blew through with a fury. Rain pounded the roof, while lightning and thunder echoed through the sky. High winds danced around trees, knocking off branches, blowing over fences, and leaving their mark all over the ground. The impact was noticed immediately; the power was off.

Tree branches lay not only across roads, on roofs, and in yards, but tangled in the power lines. Millions were without power as light company crews worked around the clock to bring energy back to our homes and businesses.

In the darkness, we learned new lessons about light. It is amazing how a few days without electricity changes your perspective. Light affects everything! The rhythm of our days followed the sun. Nighttime took on a different feel in the candlelight. Our meals revolved around what could be cooked on the grill and kept in a cooler. We smelled different since there was no way to wash and dry clothes. Even our appearance changed. Many us of look very different with electricity at our disposal than we do without!

God used these days to remind us of the power of Light. His presence in our lives should permeate everything we do. It should impact the rhythm of our days, how we sleep at night, where we go, how we talk with our neighbors, even our appearance! Moses was radiant after being in the presence of the Lord (Exodus 34:29). He shone with a heavenly light that was evident to all. The same is true with you and me. Our lives are meant to shine with the light of Christ. We may suffer occasional power failures, but our Light will never go out!

My Jesus Resolution today is to appreciate the Light. Jesus tells me that He is the Light of the world. He calls me to reflect His light. Today I am going to shine. I am going to let the light of Jesus overflow in my day. I am going to remember the darkness, and praise Him for the way He illuminates my world. I am going to share His light with someone stuck in the dark. I am going to honor the truth that without His light everything would be different.

Every time you turn on a light switch today, thank God for being your Light.

We hiked to the stream. Actually, it wasn't much of a hike and it wasn't much of a stream. Still, we had walked through the mud to a creek outside of Seattle to see the salmon running. We ambled along the curves of the stream looking for the salmon intent on making their way against the current. Finally, we found a place where the water was rushing over a fallen tree. There in the shallows of the stream, we found the salmon.

I guess that I had expected the picture to be a little more dramatic. A raging river, perhaps, with rocky boulders creating overwhelming obstacles. That is what you see in the movies anyway. Our little stream was quiet. It wasn't the kind of place where news cameras swarm or poets search for inspiration. It was ordinary, and in the ordinary I saw God's genius.

The salmon in our little stream gathered around one particular curve. Here the current was moving around a fallen tree, pushing the water forward. The salmon worked hard to hold their place. They had to maneuver to stand against the tide. You could almost see them gathering their resolve to make the push forward. One would surge ahead, only to get knocked back, sometimes several feet downstream. They didn't give up. Slowly but surely, they allowed the instinct God gave them to move them back upstream.

One fish seemed particularly determined. Holding its place in the water, the salmon seemed to ignite its energy by moving its tail back and forth. Then it plunged ahead. It made a few inches progress, then worked on maintaining its new place in the stream. I cheered, and saw myself.

God calls us to be a people who swim upstream. We may not move through dramatic waters, but He calls us to be His in the ordinary places in our lives. As His children, we are never meant to go with the flow, be swept along by the world, or take the easiest path. God calls us, like He calls the salmon, to move in a direction that brings us to His great purpose in our lives. A salmon can't fulfill its purpose if it doesn't make the journey upstream. Neither can we.

My Jesus Resolution today is to set my eyes on swimming upstream. I am not going to let the world define my direction or set my path. I am going to go where God calls me, even if it means moving in the opposite direction of those around me. I might get knocked back. I might expend energy just holding my place in the current. But nobody hikes through the mud to see fish swimming downstream. Maybe by swimming in my ordinary part of the stream today, I can point somebody to Jesus.

How comfortable are you with swimming upstream?

My son is taking Latin. He is learning the language, getting a glimpse of the culture, and enjoying the introduction to a foreign language. One of the first phrases he learned was *Carpe Diem* – "Seize the Day." It has become a motto for the way his teacher wants them to embrace learning.

Time is precious. It is a gift from God. Though often misused by the world, I think that the idea of seizing the day belongs to Him. The Latin word *carpe* actually means "pluck." It carries the idea of picking fruit when it is ripe.[4] Pick fruit too early, and it is hard and not very sweet. Pick it too late, and it is mushy and beginning to rot. Pluck it at just the right moment, and you have an exquisite delight.

Here are ten thing that are ripe for the picking today:

1. Seize time with God.

2. Seize the opportunity to bow your head in prayer.

3. Seize the grace He offers you.

4. Seize the reasons to rejoice He has given you.

5. Seize the chance to express gratitude and thanksgiving.

6. Seize the moment to tell someone you love them.

7. Seize joy.

8. Seize His hand and let Him pull you closer to His heart.

9. Seize the surrender to which He calls you.

10. Seize the opportunity for worship and for praise.

My Jesus Resolution today is to Seize the Day. The picture of "seizing" is one of grabbing hold of and not letting go. I want to embrace every opportunity God gives me to meet Him today. I long to experience the sweetness of His presence, and the goodness that comes from tracing His hand on my heart. I don't want this day to end with regrets. I want to seize the day, pluck the ripe fruit, and take advantage of every chance He has for me to look like Jesus.

How will you Seize the Day today?

> *For just as the body is one and has many members, and all the members of the body, though many, are one body, so it is with Christ.* — I Corinthians 12:12

Have you ever really stopped to look at your body? We are indeed fearfully and wonderfully made. Intricate systems work together to help us sleep, eat, grow, learn, and move. Most of the time we don't think about all the different parts of our bodies that are working in sync to help us wash dishes, read a book, or walk in the neighborhood. Yet each one is a gift from God and reveals His wisdom.

Paul gives us a beautiful and practical picture of the church as the body of Christ. Jesus is the head of the body. It is in Him and through Him that we have life. Just as your head guides your entire body, so Christ must lead the church. He gives it direction and purpose.

As parts of the body, we are interconnected with Christ and each other in a unique way. We do not function independently. Rather, we join together to work for a common purpose. Feet cannot function without legs; eyes are protected by eyelids; each piece is nourished by the digestive system. Each blood cell is as important as the heart that pumps those cells for neither would work without the other.

This interconnection provides us with special privileges. We are not alone. When we hurt, others know our pain. When we fall, others will help to pick us up. We stand united with the whole body of Christ. These privileges also lay a responsibility on our hearts. We are not alone. Our actions and purposes must be for the good of the whole body. Each part of the body has a function that must be fulfilled, or the entire body will suffer.

My Jesus Resolution today is to pay attention to my body. My physical body is supposed to remind me that I am a part of the body of Christ. The care I show my physical body is meant to be a reminder to be deliberate about care for the soul. Each ligament helps me see my connection to the rest of the body. Each movement reminds me to live under the authority of the Head. The body of Christ is a gift from God. It reveals His wisdom and His grace. Today I am going to thank God for the intricate way He connected us all together.

How will this picture of the body connect you more closely to Jesus today?

Excerpt from
Women Opening the Word
Paul: By the Grace of God

The Jesus Resolution
GOD WILL MAKE A WAY

I found myself humming this morning as I was walking and praying. The words to Don Moen's beautiful song, "God Will Make a Way" seemed to overflow as an answer to the concerns and requests pouring out of my heart. "God will make a way where there seems to be no way, He works in ways we cannot see, He will make a way for me."[5]

I love that thought. How many times does God make a way when all we see are obstacles, barriers, and defeat? God has a track record of opening unexpected doors, creating unanticipated paths, and working through less than obvious people. He opened a way for Abraham and Sarah. Well into their Medicare years, there seemed to be no way that God's promise of a child could be answered in their lives. Then came Isaac. God's way for Joseph led him through the bottom of wells, prison cells, and Egypt's throne rooms. The Israelites must have rubbed their eyes in wonder as they walked through a canyon made of sea water. Joshua faced big walls and big enemies, but God's way marched him around a city to victory. God's way for David proved that faith was a greater weapon than a sword. He opened a way for Daniel by closing the lions' mouths. He made a way for all of us to come to His heart by declaring "It is finished" on a cross and by opening a tomb.

I have seen it over and over in my own life. The path I never would have chosen becomes a road of great blessing. The hardship I thought would undo me became the way God unleashed His presence in my heart. The friendship I cried for but never would have found on my own. The provision He makes when all I see is the mountain. God is not limited by my vision, understanding, or resources. He will always make a way – it may not be the easy way, the fastest way, or the smoothest way – but it will be the best way. The way that leads me deeper into His love.

My Jesus Resolution today is to trust that God will make a way for me. I am going to stop fretting and start looking for the ways that He is at work around me. His answer may already be in front of me, or I may have to wait to see it unfold. The way He opens may not be the one I am looking for. I need to keep my eyes open. I must stop trying to work out my own solutions, and instead rely on the One who has proven He can handle giants, oceans, lions, and even death. God will make a way because He is the Way.

Tell someone about a time that God made a way for you.

I watched her anguish as she suffered a devastating miscarriage. Dreams slipped away, hearts broke, tears fell, and pain came in tidal waves. Holding her in those dark moments, there was nothing to say. The only comfort available was the comfort of presence.

Time passed as she made her way through dark days. Moments that were supposed to be milestones became markers of loss and places to put her heart in God's hand. She hung onto His love, committed herself to His wisdom, and struggled to embrace His good purpose for her family.

It was only a few months later that we received word of another friend walking through the same deep darkness. My friend's response surprised me. I had been worried that the news would envelop her in the pain that she had experienced, that it would all be a difficult reminder of the way her heart still ached. Instead, she flew into action. She went to our mutual friend's side and poured out God's blessings. She drew a straight line from pain to praise. She committed herself to walking with her through the loneliness and doubts yet to come.

> *Blessed be the God and Father of our Lord Jesus Christ, the Father of mercies and God of all comfort, who comforts us in all our affliction, so that we may be able to comfort those who are in any affliction, with the comfort with which we ourselves are comforted by God.* — 2 Corinthians 1:3-4

My friend lived out this verse before my eyes. She took the comfort she had been given by God and poured it as a balm on the pain of another. She told me that she found meaning in her loss as she shared her pain with another. God had comforted her. Now she was equipped to comfort someone else.

My Jesus Resolution today is to be a comforter. God has wrapped me in His comfort more times than I can count. It is a comfort that is meant to shape me into a comforter. One of the ways that God works out His purpose in us is by using every experience to draw us closer to His heart. The comfort He pours into my life is meant to overflow onto the pain of others, pointing them to Jesus, surrounding them with His love, and helping them find comfort in the greatest Comforter of all.

Who can you comfort today with the comfort you have received from God?

I am proud of my kids. They are becoming the neatest people. Each one celebrated an accomplishment this week that was worthy of bringing out the "You're Special" plate at the dinner table. We cheered, high-fived, marked the reaching of milestones, and talked about the remarkable ways God is working in each of their lives. It has been a neat week.

My pride in my kids overflows when I watch the people they are choosing to become. They have Jesus on their hearts. I hear His voice in their words. I get to see their servant hearts and stand in wonder. But the reason I am proud of my kids is not primarily rooted in what they do. I am proud of them for who they are.

I wrapped my arms around my oldest son today and told him I was proud of him. "Do you know why?" I asked. "Why?" he said. "Because you're mine," I told him.

God is proud of you. He loves who you are becoming in Him. Jesus is taking shape in your life. He delights in the way you fold your hands in prayer, open your Bible with a heart ready to meet Him, and keep a lookout for the all the ways He is present in your day. But God's delight in you is not measured primarily by your performance. He is proud of you because you belong to Him. Relationship is what connects your heart to His. You are His child. And that is enough.

My Jesus Resolution today is to delight in the delight of my Father. He loves me. Not because of what I do, but because I am His. Obedience, surrender, submission, and service are a part of my heart. They teach me about Him. They shape me to be more like Jesus. But doing more, working harder, or digging deeper won't make Him love me more. God says the same thing to me that I say to my child, "I am proud of you because you are mine."

Rest in the truth today that God is proud of you because you are His.

PATIENCE

Patience is a virtue. I am not really sure that our society has a good grasp on the meaning and importance of virtues any more. We know they are supposed to be good things, but seem a bit dusty and antiquated.

According to the dictionary, a virtue is "the quality or practice of moral excellence or righteousness." When we let God define our virtues, it is a snapshot of what it means to look like Jesus.

Patience is one of those virtues that helps frame the presence of Christ in our lives. I struggle with being patient. It requires waiting, slowing down, and putting my desires to the side while making room for God to work. Instead of being patient, I often complain about how slow people are moving, question why answers don't unfold in my timing, and wonder aloud about when things are going to align according to my perfect plan.

Recently, I was talking about patience (and my lack thereof) with a group of friends when they shared a definition that stopped me in my tracks. Patience, they explained, is waiting without whining.

Light bulbs started popping all over the place. Patience is more than suffering through the moment in order to get what I want. Patience is waiting, trusting, and depending on the goodness of God. Patience is best framed in a heart that can worship, instead of whine, while it is waiting. It declares the faithfulness, righteousness, and mercy of the Lord even before it sees answers or experiences resolution. A patient heart finds joy in the act of waiting, experiencing the presence of God in moments when I tend to whine about wasted time.

My Jesus Resolution today is to wait without whining. I am going to practice patience (and it will take practice!) I am going to see moments of waiting today as opportunities to praise Him, rather than tapping my foot and complaining. If I view those times that require patience with the expectation that God is going to do something good, I might be surprised at how God infuses those moments with His grace.

How will you practice waiting without whining today?

I am a coupon clipper. I take the coupon section out of the newspaper each week and scour the ads for coupons that will save us a few cents. We look for specials, save flyers that offer promotions, and take advantage of sales. It all adds up in helping us to be good stewards of the blessings God has poured into our lives.

Right now I am holding a twenty dollar coupon for my favorite bookstore. Bookstores are my favorite places on earth so this is a special treat. I can't wait to go. I can look, browse, peek into chapters, examine covers, and buy something that will open the door to an adventure of the heart and mind. There is a lot of fine print on the coupon, but I am sure I will find a way to use it. It is twenty dollars, after all.

My coupon makes me think of God's best deal. He doesn't offer cents-off coupons, promotional specials, or a super low price to lure me into buying something bigger and better. His deal is simple – it's free.

For by grace you have been saved through faith. And this is not your own doing; it is the gift of God. — Ephesians 2:8

Grace is a gift. It is free. Freely given from the heart of God, paid for by the love of God, poured out into our lives by the mercy of God. There is no amount of hard work that will get you more grace. You can't bargain or get a preferred customer's discount. Everyone who accepts grace must accept it as a free gift from God.

It sounds easy enough, but we make it so difficult. A free gift means I didn't do it by myself. It requires I admit I need a gift as big as grace. Too many times I try to find my own way to earn grace, rather than accepting it as the gift it is meant to be. I want to add fine print, when all God asks is that we accept what He longs to give us.

My Jesus Resolution today is to open my heart to the grace God wants to give me. I am going to let grace humble me today. I want the generosity of God's gift to penetrate the hard places in my heart. I long for the free nature of His grace to open my eyes to all the other things He wants to give me. His gift inspires me to give myself completely to Him. Grace isn't found in the fine print. Grace is best seen in a Savior who writes "FREE" with His blood on a cross.

Be amazed by amazing grace today.

The Jesus Resolution

HEAVEN-ALL-YEAR-ROUND

I went to a special shop this weekend. It was a Christmas-all-year-round store. It was a beautiful shop that was filled with nooks and crannies that were just made to explore. Around each corner was a new Christmas tree with its own unique theme and decorations. The shop was filled with the lights, sounds, and smells of Christmas. Definitely the kind of place that fills you with the Christmas spirit and a desire for the season to hurry up and arrive.

As I retrace my steps in my memories, I realize that our lives should be like this shop. Heaven-all-year-round. Our hearts should glow with the lights of heaven. Our lives should sparkle with the beauty of heaven. Each one of us presents heaven's theme in our own unique way while still being unified by one common tie. We should be the kind of people that fill others with a desire for heaven to hurry up and get here.

Some people roll their eyes at the idea of a store being dedicated to one day. Some people will look at us and shake our heads at devoting our lives to one truth. Just smile at them and invite them in. We know that heaven will be here quicker than we think and it will be more wonderful than we can imagine.

My Jesus Resolution today is to imagine a life devoted to heaven-all-year-round. What would my life look like if I were dedicated to showcasing the beauty of heaven here on earth? Would I sing more and complain less? Would I lift my eyes from the worries of this world to the wonder of His love? Would I dedicate my time to removing what doesn't fit the heaven theme, filling my heart with the fruit of His presence instead? A heaven-all-year-round life showcases Jesus around every turn. That's who I want to be because that is where I want to go.

How can you make today a heaven-all-day kind of day?

I just got off the phone with my daughter. I love talking to her. She is away at school and doing well. She calls every day and we talk. Sometimes it is just for a few minutes. Just a moment to touch base and connect with home. Other days find us on the phone for a long time. There are struggles to talk about, heartache to pray over, encouragement to be given, and laughter to be shared. I look forward to hearing her voice every time.

I am thankful for the way we talk and how it binds our hearts together. Sometimes she calls to say something silly. This last week, there was a call to share deep sorrow. Some days she is down and needs encouragement, a pep talk, or a cheerleader. Other times, she just needs a hug or a laugh or a reminder that home is not as far away as it seems.

Prayer is a lot like calling home. It opens the door and allows us to connect to God. In prayer, we pour out our hearts and allow God to pour Himself into us. We share our thoughts, hurts, desires, and struggles, and ask God to shape how we see our days. We can talk to Him about what we find discouraging, disheartening, and dismaying. Prayer can also be filled with laughter, thanksgiving, and joy. In prayer, God reminds us that home is not as far away as it sometimes seems.

My Jesus Resolution today is to "call home." I am going to be intentional about talking to my Father, sharing my heart, and delighting in the connection that prayer provides. It is okay if I want to call about something silly. I can go to Him if I need to share heartbreak and tears. My daughter has taught me to see that time on the phone through God's eyes. I delight in the conversation, whatever it may be. God delights in the time you spend talking together as well. Call home today. Someone is waiting to hear your voice.

Read Isaiah 65:24.
When will you call on God today?

NATIONAL DREAM DAY

I saw it on a tag. I thought it said "National Dream Day," and I got really excited. It didn't. I misread it, but it sparked my thinking. What a neat idea! What if there really was a National Dream Day? A day set aside to dream about the future, let hope expand, and allow our imaginations to take flight? What would you dream about?

In days filled with deadlines, obligations, appointments, and laundry, dreaming often moves into the realm of wishful thinking. If we had time, we would… When there is more money, we will… If only…

Dreaming, however, is essential to the abundant life. God created us to dream – big! He wants us to stretch our hearts and imagine a world vibrant with His presence. He longs for us to plunge into the depths of His love and soak in all the possibilities He has in store for us. He dreams of a kingdom filled with people transformed to look like His beloved Son.

When we dream, we lift our eyes from the boundaries of our present reality to the face of God. In our dreams, we are not limited by the here and now, by the naysayers who tell us it can't be done, or by the limited resources that so often define who we are. When we dream, we can imagine a world touched by grace, infused with goodness, and bound together by love.

God has bigger dreams in mind for us than we can possibly imagine. He has plans for us that can only be fueled by His power and ignited by His mercy. Abraham dreamed of a family. God used him to bless all nations. David dreamed of building a temple. God raised up a house for the coming Messiah. Peter dreamed of catching fish. Jesus transformed Him into a fisher of men.

But Jesus looked at them and said, "With man this is impossible, but with God all things are possible." — Matthew 19:26

My Jesus Resolution today is to take time to dream. I am not going to be afraid to dream impossible dreams or pray for big things. I am going to let my dreams lift my eyes to His face. I am going to embrace the dreams I know God is already working out in my life. I am going to imagine how life might look if the power of God was fully unleashed in my life. I am going to let that dream stretch my soul and fuel my surrender. I declare today to be National Dream Day. I dare you to dream a God-sized dream.

What God-sized dream will you dare to dream today?

FILTERED WATER

We drink a lot of water at our house. Plenty of water is necessary for good health, so we keep a pitcher in our refrigerator full of water to encourage everyone to drink up. It is one of those pitchers with a built-in filter. Every day, sometimes more often, we stand by the sink and fill up the pitcher. As soon as the water runs through the filter, we have delicious drinking water available for everyone.

The filter on the pitcher has a very specific purpose. The water doesn't flow into the main compartment of the pitcher until it passes through the filter. The purpose of the filter is to extract all the impurities and junk in the water. It takes time for the water to move through the filter. Drop by drop it falls into the pitcher different from how it came out of the tap. Clean, pure, and delicious, the filtered water is ready for us to drink.

Watching the water flow through the filter into the pitcher gives me an insight into how God wants us to guard our hearts and minds. Too many times, I let the world flow straight into my heart. Polluted and unclean, it goes into my system, bringing its impurities with it.

Instead, God wants me to filter what comes from the world before it goes into my heart and mind. He has given us a holiness filter to process all the junk out, and let in all the goodness He has in store for us.

But the fruit of the Spirit is love, joy, peace, patience, kindness, goodness, faithfulness, gentleness, self-control; against such things there is no law. — **Galatians 5:22-23**

God gives us His Spirit to help us filter out the impurities of the world. What things will help us grow into His likeness? The fruit of the Spirit becomes a good filter to measure whether something is going to help us look like Jesus. Does it encourage love? Does it foster peace? Does it promote patience and kindness? Does it honor goodness and faithfulness? Does it celebrate gentleness and self-control? Things that go through this filter pass the test and help us become spiritually healthy.

My Jesus Resolution today is to use God's filter. I am not going to let the world's junk fill my mind with its impurities. I want to grow to look like Jesus. In order to do that, I need the best nourishment I can get. God has a filter in place for me. If I will take the time to let everything run through it, I will be able to fill myself with the pure Living Water.

How will you use God's filter today?

We tend to view our own lives as ordinary. We look at the people around us and can clearly see the way God is using them to spread the light of His love. One may shine His light as a teacher. Another wraps light around your heart with encouragement and love. There may be someone who through service and graciousness brings light to the darkness. As you bask in the light of God that radiates through these special people, it is often difficult to recognize that God can and does use your life, your heart, and your talents to reflect the light of His glory.

God uses ordinary, regular people to shine the light of His grace into this dark world. That is good news for you and me!! As we look into the pages of His Word, it is especially tempting to believe that God's heroes of faith were somehow different, special, and uniquely qualified to stand up and be counted as lights for God. The life of Elijah shows us the truth of how God uses people for His service.

Elijah was a man with a nature like ours…— James 5:17a

Wait a minute! This is Elijah we are talking about here. He rose up to be the most powerful prophet that ever worked among the nation of Israel in the Old Testament. He stood alone against an idolatrous queen and called the people back to the pure worship of Jehovah. The spirit and power of Elijah were said to define the ministry of John the Baptist. Elijah stood beside Jesus as He brilliantly shown on the mountain during His transfiguration. That Elijah, James tells us, was just like us.

Your life becomes an extraordinary testimony to the awesome power of God when you give yourself over to His service. That is what

Elijah did. He was just like us — he was a regular, ordinary man. Through him however, God did miraculous things because he was willing to be used by the Master. He didn't let his being "ordinary" stop him. Rather he let God's power shine through his life as a witness to the faithfulness and holiness of the Lord. God longs for you to make the same commitment to usefulness.

My Jesus Resolution today is to rejoice in the ways God uses the ordinary. I don't have to be special, super talented, have all the answers, or be able to leap tall buildings in a single bound. I have to put myself in the hands of God. He takes it from there, turning ordinary me into something extraordinary – the image of Jesus.

How does the way God used ordinary Eljiah frame the way He wants to work in your life?

Excerpt from
Women Opening the Word
A Light in the Darkness: Elijah and Elisha

NEW BOOKS

I just bought some new books. I am so excited. I love new books. I love to read. There is something so engaging about joining characters in an adventure that helps me explore my heart.

Thumbing through my new books brought my heart to the sixty-six books I too often take for granted. In these sixty-six books are the most exciting stories ever written. They capture the essence of our journey, the deepest needs of our hearts, the wonder of living a life bigger than we can imagine, and the wisdom to show us how to take the next step.

The stories in the Bible may be familiar ground, but they are ever new. That is one of the unique and demanding characteristics of His Word. *"For the word of God is living and active, sharper than any two-edged sword, piercing to the division of soul and of spirit, of joints and of marrow, and discerning the thoughts and intentions of the heart"* (Hebrews 4:12).

All other books fall flat when compared to the Bible. He uses each word to open my eyes to His character, to call me into deeper holiness, to touch my heart and heal my pain, to challenge me to sacrifice and draw me into more complete surrender. The stories laid out in its pages are meant to inspire, provoke, challenge, encourage, and shine a light deep into who I am. They are meant to showcase His goodness, spotlight His power, underscore His love, and explain His purposes. Every word of every page tells me about Jesus and the transformation He longs to work in my life. The more I devote myself to reading it, the more like Him I become.

My Jesus Resolution today is to read God's Word with joy. I want to pick up my Bible with the same enthusiasm as I do a new book. God has a story to tell me. It is a story about His love, His Son, and His plan for me. Now that's a story I want to dive into.

Pray for new eyes, a fresh heart,
and an open mind today as you read
God's Word.

VISITORS

We stopped at the gate. From the very beginning, our car was tagged as different. Visiting my parents, we moved over into the lane designated for guests and parked at the entrance to their neighborhood. Residents fly through the gated entrance. Visitors are required to stop and check in.

The guard came out in his official uniform, carrying his even more official looking clipboard. He wrote down our license plate number and asked why we wanted access to the streets just beyond the gate. We explained our connection to one of their residents, and he gave us a tag, waving us through the entrance.

For the rest of our visit, we were required to carry a tag that boldly named us as "visitors." Wherever we went, whatever part of the neighborhood we drove in, while we settled in at my parent's house, everyone who passed by knew, without a doubt, that we were visitors. We didn't belong there. We didn't live there. This wasn't our home. We were visitors.

For the neighborhood, those visitor tags are a matter of security. Looking at the tag, I sometimes wish they were required for Christians. We are visitors in this world—guests, travelers, people passing through. This is not our home. We don't live here. We don't belong in this world. Peter tells us to "...*conduct yourselves with fear throughout the time of your exile*" (I Peter 1:17). I need a ready reminder that I am just a visitor here. My home is elsewhere. I don't need to get too comfortable, invest too much, or stake my claim in a neighborhood that is never meant to be my residence.

My Jesus Resolution today is to remember that I am a visitor. This world is a wonderful place to visit, but it isn't my home. I want to enjoy my stay, but always keep my heart hungry to go to the place I truly belong. It is okay if the world knows I am a visitor. I don't have to fit in, follow the crowd, or abide by its standards. Sometimes I need to be reminded that I am just a visitor. I think I will keep that visitor tag in my car for a little while longer.

What reminder will you carry with you today to help you remember that you are a visitor?

HERE-SICKNESS

There is a story about a little boy away from home for the first time. Missing his mom and dad, the people around the little boy asked him if he was homesick. The little boy shook his head, gazing at the others with that look only little boys have when they know the right answer and wonder why everyone else can't see it. "I'm not homesick. I am here sick."

Do you ever get here-sick? Do you ever miss home so much you think your heart is going to break? Ever just feel overwhelmed for the sights, sounds, and nearness of those who make home home? We call it homesickness, but we aren't sick of home. We are sick of here. Here has lost its appeal. Here doesn't meet the needs of our hearts. Here is not home.

Christians should have an increasing case of here-sickness. As we take on more and more of the image of Christ, we should increasingly feel like we don't fit in this world. Our walk with God should make us ache for home. To be in the place where we know we truly belong. To be with the One whose arms are truly our refuge and sanctuary.

My Jesus Resolution today is to think a little bit more about home. I can't wait to see Jesus' face. My knees long to fall in His presence. My hands ache to touch the hem of His garment. My throat tightens thinking about the songs of praise I want to sing. The little boy is right. I am not homesick. Home is where I want to be. Home is where I want to stay. Home is where my heart feels most, well, at home. I am here-sick, and I can't wait to go home.

Read Revelation 4:1-11.
Let it fuel your thoughts of home today.

The Jesus Resolution
A LESSON IN CONTENTMENT

Another lesson from the car seat. My preschool friend and I were driving to school this morning. He announced in the driveway that we would be looking for dump trucks, cherry pickers, and school buses. Keeping our eyes open and paying attention to all the neat things God puts in our path is one of our greatest joys.

Our eyes were peeled and almost immediately he saw a school bus. Smiles exploded from the backseat as he noted how quickly we were spotting these road treasures. Driving along, he noticed a bright yellow car and pointed it out. I told him that it was a fun car, and that I would like to have a car like that one. He got a puzzled expression on his face. "But you already have a car."

I do have a car. Of course, I couldn't learn my lesson on the first go around. I tried explaining that sometimes it was fun to think about what kind of car you might like to have someday. So I asked him, "Do you ever think about what kind of car you would like to have?" "No," he responded. "I just want to be four."

Contentment is the attitude of being at peace amid your circumstances. It counts the blessings that we often overlook. It sees the presence of God in the ordinary.

Too often I wish my life away. I wish for a new car rather than being thankful for what I am driving. I wish I was in a different stage of life rather than enjoying the moment I am in. I wish I was starting, or done, or had the chance to do it all over again rather than savoring the part of the journey I am on.

My Jesus Resolution today is to cultivate contentment. I am going to be satisfied with the richness of today. I am going to spend less time wishing and more time counting my blessings. I am going to keep my eyes open, looking for the treasures God puts along the road today. I am going to let every yellow car I see today remind me of the lesson of contentment God wants to plant deep in my heart.

Read Philippians 4:11-13. How will these words help you cultivate contentment today?

The Jesus Resolution

PINK CLOUDS

They were streaked across the sky. Wispy clouds painted across the deep blue of early morning. I was out walking just as the sun came peeking over the horizon. The shimmer of the starlit sky began to give way to the golden hues of the sunrise. The canopy stretching across the heavens gently framed the new morning, adding sunlight to the symphony of color playing across the sky.

I turned the corner and caught my breath. There, enmeshed in the soft blue sky of the morning, were pink clouds. Stunning colors embedded in the unfolding drama of the dawn. Painted in the clouds was every shade of pink you can imagine. Soft, pale hues were set against dark, dramatic pinks. They lit up the sky, framing a dramatic beauty that would only last for a few moments as the sun strolled over the horizon.

"He did that for me." That was the thought that captured my imagination. Understand that it was very early. The streets in my neighborhood were still sleepy and quiet. Very few others were out and about. With no one else watching, He painted beauty in the sky so I could catch a glimpse of His glory.

I am so glad that I noticed. I am so thankful to serve a God who will create wonders just to see us smile. He is more than willing to put pink clouds in the sky so that I will have another reason to praise Him and bend my heart before His throne. We don't serve an it-will-do, let-them-just-get-by God. We are loved by a willing-to-go-over-the-top Father who can't wait to amaze us with His passion for us.

My Jesus Resolution today is to look for pockets of beauty. They are scattered throughout my day. Little reservoirs of glory meant to draw my eyes to His face. Too many times I walk on past, not paying attention, content to focus on my list, my agenda, my struggles, and my stuff. Today, however, I am going to look up and pay attention to the beauty He is planting in my day. He gave me pink clouds. Imagine what He has in store for you.

Read Luke 8:39.
What has God done for you today?

INTERRUPTIONS

She didn't know she was interrupting. I was in the middle of a meeting, and someone came in to talk. My coworker graciously opened up the time to answer her questions. I sat in the other room stewing about being interrupted.

I don't like interruptions. I make plans, set agendas, work timelines, and organize my calendar so I can get it all done. Interruptions slow me down. They get in my way. They disrupt the flow of my day. And so often, God uses them as reminders that it isn't all about me.

God uses interruptions to refocus my attention. His plan should be my priority. His timing should be my delight. His rhythm should rule my days. God uses interruptions to redefine my priorities, to reshape my thinking, and to pull my heart back to Him.

I am slowly learning to see interruptions as holy moments. I began to pray for the woman in the other room. I wanted to cross another item off my to-do list, but God was opening a door for someone to see Jesus. In interrupting my schedule, He was teaching me about surrender. In watching my friend, I learned much about moving in the movement of God.

My Jesus Resolution today is to be thankful for interruptions. Instead of getting irritated, I am going to start looking for the movement of God in the moment. I am going to see the interruption as a yellow light to slow down and pay attention. Jesus was interrupted by people all the time. He saw each interruption as an opportunity to point someone to the face of His Father. I want to be like Jesus. I want my life to be about His timing, His will, and His movement. So today, I am going to be thankful when He interrupts me in order to pull my eyes back to His heart.

How might God be using interruptions to pull your eyes to His heart?

SCARY FAITH

You could hear the giggles echoing all over the house. My son was playing with a preschooler and the laughter was contagious. I dried my hands, stepping from the kitchen to the family room to see what was producing such joy.

My son, a high school student, was crouched on the floor in a football stance. The little guy squealing so infectiously was setting up to launch himself across the room. My son dug in, bracing himself for the "tackle" that was about to come. Our little friend started a full-scale run straight into the outstretched arms awaiting him. A few feet from his target, he vaulted straight into the sky – arms wide open, feet sailing behind him – flying through the air. My son caught him. There were hugs, tickles, and more giggles, and then the routine started all over again.

My son caught my eye, marveling at our little friend's complete trust. "He just knows I will catch him every time," he said as he prepared for another tackle. "That is a picture of faith in action," I replied. "Yeah," my son noted, "scary faith."

Scary faith. I like that. Not scaredy-cat faith, not timid faith, not weak faith – scary faith. Faith willing to take risks. Faith willing to fly. Faith so confident in the One who is holding us that we are willing to launch ourselves from across the room just to land in His arms. Faith willing to leave the ground in order to experience joy.

Paul put it this way in 2 Timothy 1:7 – *"for God gave us a spirit not of fear but of power and love and self-control."*

My Jesus Resolution today is to take a step in scary faith. I am going to move out of my comfort zone and into the arms of God. I am going to relinquish control and let Him take the lead. I am going to take a risk, trusting that He will catch me. I am going to surrender when it doesn't seem logical. The world may shake its head. It may try to discourage me or dissuade me from running and making the leap. But the world doesn't know what I know – His arms are open wide and He is waiting for me to fly.

How will you take a leap of scary faith today?

I am not a math whiz. I never did think that acute triangles were all that cute. I value the discipline of mathematics, but can't say that it was a subject that brought me great joy.

There was one line of math problems, however, that did inspire a light bulb to shine over my head – greater than and less than. Once I got the direction of those two-sided triangles figured out, it all clicked. I could look at two numbers, insert a sideways "v," and find the solution.

John 3:30 has one of these kind of math problems in it. It is a story problem in which some disciples are trying to balance the equation, but John the Baptist teaches them about greater than and less than. His disciples are troubled by swelling crowds and diminishing attention. John looks at Jesus and says, *"He must increase, but I must decrease."*

Greater than and less than. John keeps his eyes on Jesus and comes up with the right answer. I must continually have more of Jesus in me and less of self. Jesus must grow bigger in my life. He must take preeminence. He must loom large while self moves into the grave.

The interesting part of the equation is joy. In the sentence before John reveals the greater than/less than answer, he states, *"Therefore this joy of mine is now complete."* When Jesus is greater than and I am less than, the result is complete joy.

My Jesus Resolution today is to work the math problem. My dad was right – I really will use this stuff later in life. Today, understanding greater than and less than will help me see the importance of more Jesus and less me. It will help me keep the sideways "v" pointed in the right direction. I want to be like John, keeping my eyes on Jesus and helping others find the solution in Him.

Create a math equation that shows the balance of your relationship with Jesus.

BENEATH THE CROSS OF JESUS

Back in 1872, Elizabeth Celphane penned the words to the beautiful and now much-loved hymn "Beneath the Cross of Jesus." As its familiar melody plays through your mind, remember the words of the last verse of Elizabeth's song.

> *I take, O cross, thy shadow for my abiding place;*
> *I ask no other sunshine than the sunshine of His face;*
> *Content to let the world go by, To know no gain nor loss,*
> *My sinful self my only shame, My glory all the cross!*[6]

Go back and slowly read the words to this beautiful hymn again – really let them sink in.

The question with which we must begin is this – are you living in the shadow of the cross? So many times we sing our songs with half an ear and listen to the gospel in the same way. It is easy for our hearts to become dulled when the shadow of the cross is a daily reality. We move in and out of the cross' shadow in the same way that we walk through the doors in our houses. We remember the cross on Sundays, but often times, don't let it impact our lives as we go to the store or make dinner with our families.

The cross should cast a long shadow over every aspect of our lives. The paradox is that living in the shadow of the cross means that we live in perfect light – the light of the Savior's love. Anything in our lives that is not defined by the shadow of the cross, not transformed by our relationship with the Lord, lies in the shadow of the world and thus in true darkness.

My Jesus Resolution today is to sing "Beneath the Cross of Jesus." I want it to be the anthem of my heart. I want to position my soul in the cross' shadow, letting the full light of His love burn away the darkness that tends to accumulate there. I want to listen to the story of the cross with new ears, see it with open eyes, and be moved by it in fresh ways.

Sing "Beneath the Cross of Jesus" out loud today.

Excerpt from
Women Opening the Word
The Shadow of the Cross

THE BRANCH

We had a storm this week. High winds gusted through the trees, knocking down branches. They were scattered across the ground, broken and disconnected from the trees that once gave them life.

I didn't see anybody out in their yards trying to mend the branches. No one was attempting to glue them back into place or tie them together. People were putting the broken branches into the trash. Everyone understood the basic truth of branches and their trees. Stay connected and live. Break off and you die.

This is the same picture that Jesus draws for us in John 15:4 when He says, *"As the branch cannot bear fruit by itself, unless it abides in the vine, neither can you, unless you abide in me."* Jesus tells us that He is the Vine. He is the root and source of all life. When we are connected to Him, we can grow, thrive, and be fruitful. Apart from Him, we wither and die. Branches just cannot exist apart from the vine. They cannot flourish unless they receive the life-giving, life-sustaining nourishment. The vine provides all the branches need.

There is a beautiful verb in this picture that Jesus paints for us – *abide*. Abiding is our greatest responsibility. Jesus wants our hearts to stay connected to His. When we abide, we determine to rest in Him. We take up a position next to His heart and stay there. Abide is not a passive activity. The world is constantly trying to pull us off on our own. Every day requires us to make the deliberate decision to abide in Him.

My Jesus Resolution today is to abide. I am going to stay connected to the Vine. I don't want to be like one of those branches I saw lying on the ground, lifeless and broken. I want to thrive because of His grace, and allow the fruit of His presence to fully develop in my life. Today I am going to stick to Jesus. I can do that because He has promised to stick to me.

How will you abide in Him today?

THE ADVENTURE

Jesus said that we must become like little children. The older I get, the more profound that truth becomes.

We were walking him home. Our little friend lives around the corner. He had been at our house playing, laughing, and being loved. It was time to deliver him back to his mom and dad, so we packed up his stuff and headed down the street.

My husband and I were focused on moving from point A to point B. It was time to get from one place to another. Our little friend had a different perspective. The walk home was an opportunity for adventure.

Heading down the driveway, his eyes began to sparkle with all the possibilities inherent in the journey. He decided that he would jump over every crack in the sidewalk. Not a little hop, mind you. A stop, set-your-focus, give-yourself-a-pep-talk kind of jump. He encouraged himself to jump high. He told himself he could do it. He made sure that we all cheered when he made it. And then he ran to the next sidewalk crack so he could do it all over again.

He noticed all the ordinary things that turn a walk into an adventure. Sprinklers were fascinating. Barking dogs were talking just to him. The street corner became a moment to hold hands and boldly go forward. All too soon we were home. Dad's big hug became the prize for taking the risk and going on the adventure.

My Jesus Resolution today is to have an adventure. I am going to walk somewhere today; I might as well walk with joy. I need to let my heart come alive with all the possibilities God has for me on the journey. I want to notice all the extraordinary blessings bound up in the ordinary things around me. I want to experience the grand prize of running into my Father's arms. Today holds an opportunity for adventure.

Are you ready to go on an adventure today?

CAVITIES

We are on the way to the dentist this morning. A recent checkup revealed the presence of a couple of cavities. Despite faithful brushing and flossing, those little cavities now threaten the health of someone I love.

In the grand world of dentistry, cavities are not a big deal if they are caught early. It requires an extra trip to the dentist, some time, discomfort, and expense, but it can be remedied. The dentist puts a filling in place and we can go back to our activities, but the tooth is left with a reminder of the invasion.

Cavities in our teeth work in the same way sin works in our souls. Sin worms its way in, many times without us even realizing it has taken hold in our lives. God's Word, the Spirit's work in our hearts, and spiritual friendships all provide mirrors for us to see the invasion. Checked regularly and caught early, the damage is minimal. Left unchecked, giant holes begin to eat away at our core.

Brushing and flossing are tools against cavities in our mouths. God gives us tools to help sin from building up in our lives. Worship, prayer, Bible study, quietness, service, and connection with fellow Christians all work together to provide a defense against sin. We all understand the importance of brushing our teeth every day. We teach our children to do it from the time they are very young. Investing ourselves daily in these spiritual disciplines works in our hearts in the same way brushing works on our teeth.

There is one more absolutely essential piece to good dental health – you have to see the dentist. He is the expert. He sees things we don't see. He uncovers the problems, diagnoses solutions, and steps in to heal the damage. Jesus tells us in Mark 2:17, *"Those who are well have no need of a physician, but those who are sick. I came not to call the righteous, but sinners."* Spending time in the presence of the Great Physician is the best antidote to sin. He will uncover it, cure it, and pay the bill. He will move in our lives and transform our hearts so we will be a little more resistant to sin the next time, if we will just settle in and let Him work on us.

My Jesus Resolution today is to take time for a checkup. I am going to sit down in His presence and open my heart. I want His Word to shine brightly into the crevices of my life. I want to be transparent with my friends, so they can help me see what needs the touch of Jesus. The best part is that when Jesus takes care of the sin in my life, it isn't a patch job or a filling. He gives me a fresh start with a brand new heart. One He is shaping to look just like Him.

Make an appointment for a checkup with the Great Physician.

ADOPTION

Adoption is a special word. It frames a heart that longs for relationship and is willing to go the extra mile to bring someone close to itself. A willingness to share life, bestow love, deepen connection, and unveil a mystery are all wrapped up in that single word.

We got just a little taste of the joy and wonder of adoption as we stood in line at the animal shelter. We looked at dog after dog, each needing love, some TLC, and a home. Big puppy dog eyes met us at each turn. Each little face just wanted to be wanted.

We finally picked out a sweet dog and began filling out the paper work to take him home and make him a part of our family. There were questions to answer, information to gather, and commitments to make. My husband and I were interviewed to see if we were qualified to be good pet parents. The face to watch, however, was my son's. As soon as we had settled on our pup, my son never left his side. He planted himself by the kennel, leash and collar in hand, and waited. He talked to his new friend, reassuring him that life would soon be different. He anxiously watched us for a sign that the dog now belonged completely to us. He opened his heart and let Jack in. The shelter workers were amused. I saw God in my son's face.

> *...even as he chose us in him before the foundation of the world, that we should be holy and blameless before him. In love he predestined us for adoption as sons through Jesus Christ, according to the purpose of his will.* — **Ephesians 1:4-5**

God adopts us. He walks through the suffering, tragedy, and scars of this world and declares that He wants us all. He paid the price, worked through all that was required, and claimed us as His own.

He opens His heart and commits Himself to giving us a home and a place to belong. He plants Himself by our sides, reminding us each day that life is different because we are a part of his family.

My Jesus Resolution today is to rejoice in my adoption. I don't belong to this world. I belong to Jesus. I am a part of His family – loved, cherished, cared for, and valued. He welcomes me in and opens His heart to me. Just like Jack, there is some training and discipline to be had in order to best learn how to live in this new home. Today I am going to look in the mirror and let Him remind me how much I am wanted. He adopted me, and that is reason enough to rejoice today.

What special picture does adoption paint for your heart?

THANKFULNESS IN THE MORNING

Gratitude is an attitude. It is a mindset that is on the lookout for the myriad of ways God is constantly moving in our lives. When our eyes are open, our hearts are more sensitive to the presence of Christ.

I decided to challenge myself to find 10 reasons to be thankful in the first 10 minutes I was awake this morning. It was a decision to set my heart on God as I start my day. I am praying that opening my eyes to His presence first thing in the morning will cascade into an ever-increasing awareness of Him throughout my day. Here is what I am thankful for so far:

1. Quilts
2. Toothpaste
3. Warm sweatshirts
4. Good morning hugs
5. The sunrise
6. Work I love
7. A day filled with possibilities
8. Cold water
9. Apples
10. My Bible

It didn't take long. As soon as I opened my eyes, I was overwhelmed by the blessings that fill my life. They say that how you spend the first 10 minutes of your morning sets the tone for the entire day. Looking for God in these first few minutes has the power to open my eyes to His presence as I walk through each hour of my day.

My Jesus Resolution today is to be overwhelmed by gratitude. He is here. He is moving in my day. He has filled my life with more blessings that I can count. Each one is a reminder to look for His hand, trust His heart, and follow His lead. If this is what I found in the first 10 minutes, imagine how amazed I am going to be as I move through the next 1,430 minutes of the day.

Take the 10 blessings in 10 minutes challenge. What are the blessings that you find as you start your day?

PRAYING WITH A CHILD

Have you ever prayed with a little one? It is an eye-opening experience. I love to listen to children pray. Their faith shines through their prayers. The reality of God's presence is cemented in the way they pour their hearts out before Him. Their honesty challenges me to check my masks at the door and come before His throne utterly transparent. It is in their prayers laced with thanksgiving that I find myself humbled.

Here is the scene – the dinner table. You and your family are gathered around the table for a meal together. Food is on the table, the chairs are full, everyone is hungry, and it is time to pray. We bow our heads, close our eyes, and the little one wants to say the prayer. We encourage our little ones to pray aloud because that is how they learn.

The prayer starts off in the regular way. "Thank you for the chicken, fruit, but not really the green beans." Next he starts naming the people at the table, thanking God for those he loves. Then there is a long pause. At this point everyone is ready to say "amen" and dig in. Instead, a new list of thanksgiving begins. "Thank you for the forks, and the spoons, and the napkins." He thanks God for the salt and pepper, the pan on the stove, and the magnets on the refrigerator. You finally take a peek because he is thanking God for the glasses, the soap by the sink, and is starting to name the toys lying on the floor in the family room.

That is when you see it. His eyes are wide open. He is cataloguing the blessings he sees all around him. And he will keep going. Now is when someone usually speaks up with an "In Jesus name" in order to encourage the "amen" so we can move on with dinner. I wish I had never done that.

My Jesus Resolution is to keep my eyes open. My little one taught me a lesson I need to learn over and over again. I need to keep my eyes wide open when I pray. Not physically, but with my heart. There are so many blessings I miss because I am in a rush, focused on myself, or just don't see. I need to slow down, take a look around the room, and be thankful for all of the spoon, napkin, and salt and pepper blessings God puts in my life.

How will you keep your eyes open when you pray today?

She is ninety years old and the sweetest woman you would ever want to meet. Her gentle spirit speaks to long years of walking with God. She radiates a beauty that she is completely unaware she has. Her Bible is well worn. Its words are written on her heart, deeply etched from spending so much time with the Master. Her hands are stiff with arthritis, but pliable in the hands of her Lord. She serves with love, sings with joy, and inspires us with her faith and constant presence.

That is why it was so surprising. It was Sunday morning. The sermon was over, and the song we were singing invited tender hearts to deep surrender. There was a rippled pause as my sweet friend slowly made her way to the front. It was the walk of someone deeply broken, carrying a weight that only the Lord could bear. No one could imagine why she was there.

The elders surrounded her in a way that spoke to their profound respect and love for this dear soul. She talked quietly against one shoulder, bowing her head in a mirror of what was happening in her heart.

Finally, one of the elders spoke on her behalf. She had come with a heart moved to repentance and confession. She grieved her sin, longing for a fresh movement of grace. Her tender heart spoke of her deep desire to look more like Jesus and her ache that she had failed to mirror Him. She asked for forgiveness. She mourned how her actions might have impacted the hearts of those around her.

She impacted me, but not in the negative way she feared. Her tenderness broke through the hardness of my own heart. Her transparency humbled me. Her willingness to be open about her struggle cast a light on my usual desire to manage my image. Her actions of repentance and confession challenged me to examine my own actions. Her desire to look more like Jesus flamed my own deep longing.

My Jesus Resolution today is to be just like her. I want to have that kind of tender heart. I crave the sensitivity to the presence of God that she lived out before us. I long to be transparent to the core. I want to be so embedded in the movement of God that the slightest nudge sends me to my knees. I pray that someday somebody will be able to see Jesus as clearly in me as I see Him in her.

Where do you need to be more tenderhearted in your walk with God?

The Jesus Resolution

WHERE NO MAN HAS GONE BEFORE

My son loves *Star Trek*. The starship Enterprise makes regular stops at our house. He is fascinated by Spock, Captain Picard, and Klingons. The different struggles they encounter on their journeys have opened doors for conversations about how God wants us to handle those moments. The show has provided him with smiles, perspective, and new insights on how to make his own journey through life.

It is the introduction to the show that has me thinking. The show opens with an invitation to join the characters on an adventure to "boldly go where no man has gone before." Uncharted territory, new vistas, exciting encounters, and the promise to both impact and be changed by what we see is what makes the show so appealing.

If you want to watch a drama unfold about someone going where no man has gone before, the person to watch is Jesus. He is truly the only One who has boldly gone where no man has gone before. He left the glory of heaven to walk the earth as a man. He wrapped Himself in skin and took on our nature. He moved in a world He created as one of the creations. He touched our wounds. He cried our tears. He laughed with our joys. He faced our sins.

In becoming one of us, He accepted the challenge to boldly go where no man has gone before. He died on the cross, taking the full weight of my sin on Himself. He went to the grave, facing death full in the face. And then He came back, risen, triumphant, never to die again. Where no man has gone before.

My Jesus Resolution is to boldly follow Him. He made that daring journey so that I can follow in His footsteps. He went to the cross so that I could learn how to die to self. He journeyed to the grave so I would understand the necessity of being buried with Him. He rose so that I can live. He went where no man had gone before in order to open the way for me to live in His adventure.

Where do you need to more boldly follow Jesus?

AWESOME GOD

Every week he gets to pick a song. Every week he chooses the same one. His dad rolls his eyes. The people around him try to get him to pick something else. Some giggle. Some groan. I whisper a prayer of thanks. Every week he chooses "Our God Is an Awesome God."

He is just a little guy, but it is a big song with an enormous message. Our God is an awesome God. Our God is a possessive term. He is my God. We are connected. We share a relationship. We live together and walk side by side. God tells us that we can claim Him in this personal, intimate, tied-together way. *"[A]s God said, 'I will make my dwelling among them and walk among them, and I will be their God, and they shall be my people'"* (2 Corinthians 6:16b).

Our God is an awesome God. He is awesome – inspiring, impressive, excellent, and outstanding. Those are neat pictures of God's heart and His actions on our behalves. He inspires awe. He draws our hearts to worship and adoration. He inspires us to move beyond ourselves and embrace all the goodness He has for us. He is impressive and longs to impress the image of His Son deep on our hearts. He is excellent, perfect, praiseworthy, and true. His very heart becomes our standard for life and godliness. He is outstanding. There is no one like Him. He stands alone, yet opens the door for us to live with Him.

My Jesus Resolution today is to sing "Our God Is an Awesome God" out loud. I am going to let the words penetrate my soul, lift my eyes, encourage my heart, and inspire my steps. I am going to sing it until my troubles take on their proper perspective. I am going to sing it as a framework for joy. I am going to sing it for the world to hear. I can't think of a better message to let resonate in our minds than the truth that our God is an awesome God. Keep singing, little one. I will sing and smile with you.

Sing "Our God Is an Awesome God" today. Let it resonate throughout your day.

I knew it when he was very young. My son has a special heart for God. He is sensitive to the presence of God in a way that is unusual for someone just starting on this journey. He loves God with a depth that is startling. His commitment to walking in His ways has challenged me to deeper surrender. He has a servant's heart and a prophet's passion, and I am excited to see how God is going to use his life.

My first glimpse into this special relationship between God and my son came about the time he turned three. We were doing our bedtime routine and settling in for the night. The bathtub toys had been put away, teeth had been brushed, and stories had been read. We were preparing our hearts for a time of quiet prayer. I knelt by his bed, listening to his voice as he spoke to God like an old friend. We talked for a minute about faith and following Jesus, and then I kissed him good night.

A little voice followed me as I moved through the darkness. "I don't think I am going to get any Christmas presents this year." Startled, I turned around. "Of course you are. Have you been a good boy?" I asked rhetorically. A pause, and then a whispered answer, "Not all the time." That's when I saw it. A sensitivity to the things of God, a heart already responding to His call, eyes that were learning to look at Jesus, a desire for holiness born out of love and faith.

My heart was profoundly humbled. It still is. His little heart captured an awareness of His deep need for Jesus. His transparency calls me to look deeply at my own heart. Too many times I depend on my own goodness. I rely on my own knowledge, count on my own strength, and move in my own timing. I need to be reminded that being good flows from being with Jesus.

My Jesus Resolution today is to have a heart for God. I want to be so full of Jesus that there is no room for anything else. I want His love to inspire me, His holiness to penetrate me, and His power to transform me. I long to have a sensitive spirit and a quiet soul so that I can better hear His voice and respond to His call. I want to look like my son because my son already looks so much like Jesus.

Whose faith has inspired you? Thank them today for how they have looked like Jesus for you.

My mom asked me to do it. My grandparent's sixtieth wedding anniversary was approaching and my mom was collecting memories. The instruction was to write something about a precious memory I had of my grandparents.

Sorting through the memories was like looking through an old scrapbook. Pictures of childhood games, races through the grass, the click of the typewriter, and the aroma of pound cake floated through my mind. I can see my grandfather, tall and lean, sleeping on an old quilt on the laundry room floor. Pictures of my grandmother asking me to check her lipstick make me smile. But the memory that is most deeply seared in my mind is not one from my childhood. It happened when I was old enough to realize the gift they had given our family.

It was Sunday morning. I don't remember why we were all together, but together we were. Squished together on a pew at church, we were trying to make room for wiggly children, extra Bibles, and the usual "who wants to sit next to whom" shuffle. I looked down the row, and there is my memory. Four generations of my family worshipping together. Hearts turned toward God, lives committed to living in His grace, relationships bound up in His love, my grandparents had given us an enduring legacy.

Legacies are powerful things. They are what we leave behind that will shape the generations that follow us. Legacies that last, that make a difference, that open the door to faith are deliberately shaped and intentionally lived out. Legacies aren't built in a day. They are grounded in a lifetime of small choices, well-spoken words, and consistency of spirit. Building a legacy requires keeping your eyes on the future while living fully in the present.

My Jesus Resolution today is to think about my legacy. What picture of faith do I want to leave for my children and grandchildren? What am I doing today to make that legacy a reality? I want to leave a legacy that resonates with praise. I long for future generations to be able to trace the handprints of God on our family history. I want to give them a legacy so embedded in the character of Jesus that it inspires them to walk in His steps.

Read Psalm 78:4-7.
What legacy do you want to leave
for the next generation?

SEEDS EVERYWHERE

They cover the ground. Their shells make a crunching noise under my shoes. Some of the acorns are broken open, spilling their orange flesh onto the street. Some are intact and whole, waiting for soft soil. There are hundreds of them, thousands of them on the ground. You don't have to look up at the tree to know you are standing under an oak. Just look at the seeds everywhere.

The oak isn't choosy about where its acorns fall. It sends the acorns flying to the ground, trusting that the processes God put in place will help a few of them find the right conditions for growth. The tree's job is to release the seeds. God created the oak so that it would cover its path with acorns. A few of them will find a way to sprout.

As I crunched through the carpet of acorns left by the oak tree, their sheer number provided me with a mirror and a question. How many seeds am I leaving behind? Do I leave evidence of Jesus wherever I go? Can people tell by the fruit that remains that a Christian has stood here?

God calls us to be like the oak tree and leave seeds everywhere we go. The seeds are the evidence of Jesus that invite someone to seek His face, stand surrendered beneath the cross, and dance with joy before the empty tomb. Many of the seeds will get broken. Some will get carried off and hidden away. A few might find hearts hungry for Him, and God will work in the miracle we sometimes call faith.

My Jesus Resolution today is to spread my seeds. I am going to leave Jesus behind wherever I go today. I want each person I meet to walk away with a little touch of His grace, a whiff of His aroma, and a taste of His love. It means being deliberate about my example, being intentional about my words, and being purposeful about my choices. I am going to pick up an acorn and carry it in my pocket. It will be a reminder for me of how God wants to use me to plant a seed in someone's life today.

Where will you plant a seed today?

WIND

It was windy today. It was a leaf-swirling, hair-blowing, pull-your-hood-up kind of wind. It whistled through the air, blunting the warmth of the sun climbing in the sky.

Walking in the wind brought the words of Jesus to my mind. *"The wind blows where it wishes, and you hear its sound, but you do not know where it comes from or where it goes. So it is with everyone who is born of the Spirit"* (John 3:8).

Jesus uses the wind to give us a picture of the work of the Spirit in our hearts. You can't see the wind, but you can feel its effects. It moves around you, through you, and in you. It can change your course and raise your awareness. Your steps are helped or hindered depending on whether you are walking with the wind or against it. Walking with the wind propels you forward. It gives you a push in the right direction. It almost makes you feel like you are flying. Walking against the wind is daunting. It pushes you back, trying to turn your steps around. It takes extra effort and an increasing resolve to continue to walk against the wind. With every step, you have to think about putting the other foot on the ground. The wind tries to slow you down enough to think about where your next footprint will fall.

I love this picture of the wind and the Spirit. We take the wind for granted. We sometimes view it as annoyance. Living in hurricane country, I respect the power of the wind. It can be unstoppable. Today a stiff breeze reminded me to pay attention to the movement of the Spirit in my life.

My Jesus Resolution today is to deliberately move with the wind. God gives us His Spirit so that He can fill our sails and draw us closer to His heart. I can choose whether to move with the Spirit or against Him. Either way, His purpose is to move me in the direction that most looks like Jesus. He wants to propel me forward, but will push against me if that is what is required. Pay attention when you walk outside today. Whether it is a stiff wind or a gentle breeze, let it remind you of God's presence and His desire for you to notice Him.

How will you walk in the wind today?

MY MESS

I was cooking dinner. I had put a roast in the slow cooker, letting its aroma fill the house. Having made a homemade sauce, I was checking dinner's progress and making sure that the entire roast was soaking up the delicious juices. I decided to turn the roast over in order to make sure that it was cooking evenly. Big mistake.

I got the roast turned onto its edge, but couldn't get it to make a gentle transition back into the slow cooker. Splat! Sauce and juices splashed all over me, the counter, and the side of the pot. They rolled down the counters, leaving trails on the cabinet doors as they raced to the floor. The rug by the sink framed an abstract pattern that resembled modern art. My dog thought the sauce was great. I didn't think it was so great.

I got out the cleaning supplies and started to work. The smell of bleach mingled with the aroma of the meat created a less than appetizing fragrance. I mopped up the mess, wiping the counter tops, scrubbing the cabinets, and finally pushing the dog out the way so I could clean the floor.

Then I looked at my clothes. I was covered in the aftermath of my mistake. Splashes of sauce covered both sleeves, were splattered across the front of my shirt, and even managed to find a place to land on my pants. I took them into the laundry room, praying that the stain remover would get it all out.

I have stains all the time. Not cooking messes, sin stains. The grime of guilt and the stink of stubbornness find their way into the fabric of my soul all the time. Rebellion, pride, and selfishness all leave their distinctive marks on my heart. Here is the reality. I can't scrub those stains out by myself. No amount of hard work, elbow grease, or man-made cleansers will get out the blemishes. But there is good news. The blood of Jesus can and will erase every single one. I don't have to wonder if it will work. He will. His blood is the perfect antidote to my messiest mistakes.

My Jesus Resolution today is to be thankful for the cleansing that the blood of Jesus gives me. I will make messes. Sin's stains will splash all over me today, but Jesus is there ready to clean up my mess. He has exactly what it takes to make me new, clean, and fresh. The cross isn't just a piece of wood. It is the best stain remover there is.

How will you be thankful for the way Jesus makes you clean today?

GOLDEN STREETS

It sparkled in the sunlight. I was walking through my neighborhood and the dazzle of gold caught my attention. There, in the middle of the street, was a patch of gold. It turned out to be just a candy wrapper that had been pressed into the pavement by passing cars. But for just a moment, it had captured my imagination. God used it to remind me of heaven.

> *[A]nd the street of the city was pure gold, transparent as glass.*
> **— Revelation 21:21**

We sing about streets of gold, but have you ever really stopped to imagine what that is going to look like? All of the grays of our streets will give way to pathways on fire with the light of God. They will sparkle and shimmer with the radiance of His glory. Darkness will have no place even in the paving material on the streets. The roadways will be dazzling, serving to draw our eyes and hearts to the throne of our King.

As we search for His fingerprints on our days, He is preparing our eyes for the amazing reality that will one day be ours. We will see His face. The roads in heaven all lead into His presence. A place by His side is at the heart of every promise that He makes. His glory will make gold pale in comparison. The riches of this earth will look like tar and asphalt in the light of His majesty and beauty.

My Jesus Resolution today is to dream about heaven. I am going to let pictures of golden streets and pearly gates redefine how I see beauty. Today I will walk on concrete, but remember that my feet are meant to walk on streets of gold. I will let the promise of His presence open my eyes to the light of His glory. When I see something sparkle, I will let it remind me of home.

How will you dream about heaven today?

LAYING IN THE SUN

My dog loves the sunshine. Jack has only been with us a short time, but we have learned this one thing about our little dog. He is a sunshine dog. He craves the warmth of the sun. His favorite thing to do is find a place in the sun, stretch out, and soak it all in.

He has already figured out that sun comes in best through the front glass door. Every morning, he goes to the front door and waits. He just sits there until we open the door to let the light in. He looks at the sun like an old friend and finds his spot. If we open the door just a little bit, he will scrunch his body into the small amount of sunshine coming in. Opening the door all the way creates his own little piece of sunshine heaven on the floor. He stretches out and takes it all in.

Looking out the window into the backyard reveals the same joy. When he finds a patch of sunshine, he embraces it. He claims it as his own. He refuses to move out of it. He extends his little body for maximum sun absorption. It is hilarious, and humbling.

Do I crave the Son as much as Jack craves his sunshine? Am I so aware of His presence that I anticipate His appearing and time my day around when I can soak Him in? God uses Jack to teach me an important lesson. He is willing to go wherever the sunshine falls. He will stretch himself out to soak in as much sunshine as he can get. He will even fold himself into a small pretzel in order to be in the sun.

I usually want the Son, but on my terms. I want Him to rise on my time, move for my convenience, and warm me on demand. The Son regularly appears in my day. The question is whether or not I am willing to move to meet Him and whether or not I will stretch myself in order to soak Him in.

My Jesus Resolution today is to let the sun remind me to crave the Son. I am going to open the door to my heart and let Him shine through. I am going to stop and stretch myself out in His presence, soaking up all the warmth and goodness He pours into the moment. I will go where He is, even if it means changing my path or moving things in my day. I want to spend the day in the Son. Thanks, Jack.

Do you crave time in the Son?

NINETY-THREE

The end of the semester was quickly approaching and she was fretting. One class had been particularly tough. She read the textbook, took notes, did extra credit, went to study groups, and pored over charts, definitions, and protocols. Still, it was all going to come down to one final test. If she did well enough, she would move on. If not, she would have to go back to the starting line.

She added up her scores, measured how far she needed to go, and calculated the distance to her goal. "I need an 83, Mom," she said. "If I can just get an 83, everything will be okay." I did some encouraging and cheerleading, promising to pray every step of the way.

Relating our conversation to my husband later that evening, her dad listened and said, "We are going to pray for a 93, not an 83." Right then, we started praying for a 93.

During our next phone visit, I told my daughter that we were praying for a 93. "But I only need an 83," she said. "I know, but we are going to ask for more."

For days we prayed for a 93. For days, she sweated getting an 83. Finally, the moment arrived. As she checked her grades, her eyes got wide. A big grin stretched across her face as she rejoiced in crossing the finish line. Then I watched her eyes fill up with tears. "I got a 93 on the final, Mom. I got a 93."

She studied hard for her test, but I am the one who learned a lesson. How many times do I settle for merely enough when God wants to pour out immeasurably more? Too often, I am satisfied with getting by when God wants to fill me to overflowing. I long to sneak across the finish line when God offers grace and a victor's crown.

"I came that they may have life and have it abundantly" — **John 10:10b**

My Jesus Resolution today is to pray bigger. I am going to let God's power and the riches of His mercy define the boundaries of my dreams. I want to let His will stretch my imagination. I am not going to settle for just barely enough. I don't want to just get by. I want to live in His fullness, rejoice in His richness, and praise Him for His abundance. Next time I face a test, I am going to ask for a 93.

Read Ephesians 3:20.
Where do you need to pray for a 93?

A NEW HOME

My friends are buying a new house. It is a blessing for their family and we have been excited to join them in waiting, watching, and preparing for the day to arrive when they can finally call it their own.

It has been interesting to walk with them as they prepare for "closing day." As the moment draws nearer, the place where they are living now starts to be a little less "home." Pictures come off the walls, boxes are packed, stuff is sorted, and junk is thrown out. Every day they long a little more for their new home and put a little bit of heart distance between them and the place in which they are now living.

Their anticipation has sparked my thinking. I love my home. It is filled with the people I love and things that bring me comfort and joy. This home, however, is never supposed to be more than a resting place. It is a temporary stop on my journey. Everything about this home I dwell in now should be designed to point me to what is truly home. Every plate should remind me of His provision. Every picture should point me to His beauty. Every quilt should enfold me in His comfort. I should live here, but anticipate there.

> *For we know that if the tent that is our earthly home is destroyed, we have a building from God, a house not made with hands, eternal in the heavens. For in this tent we groan, longing to put on our heavenly dwelling.* — 2 Corinthians 5:1-2

My Jesus Resolution is to look at my house differently. I want each room to teach me how to dwell with Him. I want the furniture to be places where I sit at His feet and rest in His presence. I want to remember that the stuff is just stuff and to set my heart more fully on delighting in the richness of His love. Closing day is coming sooner or later. Am I ready to move?

Walk through the rooms in your house.
Imagine Jesus in each room.

PAYING BILLS

They sit in a stack on the desk. Taking a deep breath, the bill paying process begins. Pen in hand, checks are written, on-line bill paying instructions given, calculator keys punched, and the grand total is recorded. Stamps are licked and envelopes sealed. Finally, the bills are paid. For a brief moment, everything is paid in full.

Even in the moment when the balance says "paid in full", we can look around and know that we will face this task again soon. We are using electricity even as we pay the electric bill. The dishwasher hums, using water for which we will receive a bill next month. Even as we pay our bills, the debts accrue. Paid in full is a temporary state.

Paying bills gives me an insight into the depth of what Jesus has done for me. Paying bills is similar to the sacrifices offered month after month, year after year by the Israelites. Necessary to meet the moment, but incapable of ever making us debt free. Hebrews 10:1b says, *"it can never, by the same sacrifices that are continually offered every year, make perfect those who draw near."* No matter how many times they paid, there was always more that was owed.

Jesus changed everything. He paid the bill. He bore the cost for my debt. He settled the account. Going to the cross took care of my debt in a way I could never do for myself. My debt is gone. The past is paid for. The present is redeemed. The future is clear and unencumbered. The weight of sin has been lifted off my heart. "Paid in full" is my reality in Christ.

> *But when Christ had offered for all time a single sacrifice for sins, he sat down at the right hand of God,...For by a single offering he has perfected for all time those who are being sanctified.*
> — Hebrews 10:12, 14

His one perfect sacrifice paid a lifetime of debts. His journey to the cross covered a bill that had chained my heart to death. No more worrying about how to make ends meet. No more fear or shame upon realizing that this month just put me more in the hole. My future is defined by God's dreams rather than my debt.

My Jesus Resolution today is to look at my bills differently. Every time I write a check, I am going to stop and thank Jesus for paying my debt. Every bill is going to remind me of what I owe and focus my attention on the One who paid it all. Today when I get a bill in the mail, I am going to smile as I rejoice in the truth that Jesus wrote "paid in full" across my heart.

How will paying your bills help you see Jesus today?

BABY BEAR

My son has a special friend. His name is Baby Bear. Baby Bear is a small, stuffed animal. It is a rather plain looking brown bear. No bow ties, cute outfits, or distinguishing marks. It was a gift from his brother and is absolutely precious to him.

Baby Bear goes with my son everywhere. I do mean everywhere. He wraps it in his huggie (his other life necessity) and that is all he needs. He can face any situation with Baby Bear by his side. When he needs something familiar and comfortable, he reaches for Baby Bear. When he goes into a new situation, it is Baby Bear that he wants in his arms. A trip to the store, a trip to the doctor, and a trip to Nana and Poppa's all have the same requirement – Baby Bear has to go with us.

When he is hurting or upset, guess who dries the tears and changes his mood? A moment of joy is celebrated by dancing with Baby Bear. He eats dinner with Baby Bear, sleeps with Baby Bear, and would take a bath with him, if I would let him.

My son is older now, but he learned a valuable lesson from Baby Bear. Baby Bear taught him about Jesus and how to take Him with you wherever you go. I can't tell you how many times we turned around to go back and get Baby Bear. When he went to Nana and Poppa's house, the most important moment was the transfer of Baby Bear. He couldn't be without him. Do we carry Jesus with us as completely and earnestly as my son carried Baby Bear?

My Jesus Resolution today is to insist on Jesus as fervently as my son insisted on Baby Bear. I am going to make sure that I take Him with me wherever I go. I will make His presence a priority. I will go out of my way to make sure we are together. I want Him to be a part of everything I do, big or small, scary or familiar. I am going to let Him dry my tears, heal my hurts, and infuse my day with His comfort. My son would never dream of leaving Baby Bear behind. Today I am not going anywhere without Jesus.

How will you carry Jesus with you today?

ENDNOTES

1. Huxley, Thomas Henry. Quote. *Thinkexist.com*. 11 Feb. 2011.
2. Tozer, A. W. Quote. *Thinkexist.com*. 4 Feb. 2011.
3. Boatner, Edward H. "I Shall Not Be Moved." *Songs of Faith and Praise.* West Monroe: Howard Publishing Co., Inc. 1994.
4. "Carpe diem." *The Phrase Finder*. 04 Feb. 2011.
5. Moen, Don. "God Will Make a Way." 1990. *Songs of Faith and Praise.* West Monroe: Howard Publishing Co., Inc. 1994.
6. Clephane, Elizabeth. "Beneath the Cross of Jesus." 1872. *Songs of Faith and Praise.* West Monroe: Howard Publishing Co., Inc. 1994.

Take Time For Yourself and Retreat Into The Heart of God

Relax, Read, and Reflect as Casandra Martin shows us
the way into a deeper relationship with the Father.

Women Opening the Word

ABCs of a Godly Heart - 978-0-89098-300-3
Echoing His Heartbeat: the Life of David - 978-0-89098-301-0
Fragrance of Fatih: Discovering the Aroma of Christ in the Beatitudes - 0-89098-297-X
God Pass By Me: Study of the Names of God - 0-89098-257-0
Immeasurably More - 978-0-89098-303-4
A Light in the Darkness: Elijah and Elisha - 0-89098-295-3
Our Father in Heaven...Teach Us to Pray - 0-89098-298-8
Paul, By the Grace of God - 0-89098-296-1
Set Free - 978-0-89098-302-7
The Shadow of the Cross - 0-89098-262-7
That You May Believe: the Gospel of John - 0-89098-299-6

Tell Me the Story...

In this series for both men and women,
Casandra and co-author Bill Rasco
explore your favorite stories of faith
from a fresh perspective.

The Armor of God - 978-0-89098-339-3
Meeting Jesus - 0-89098-338-0